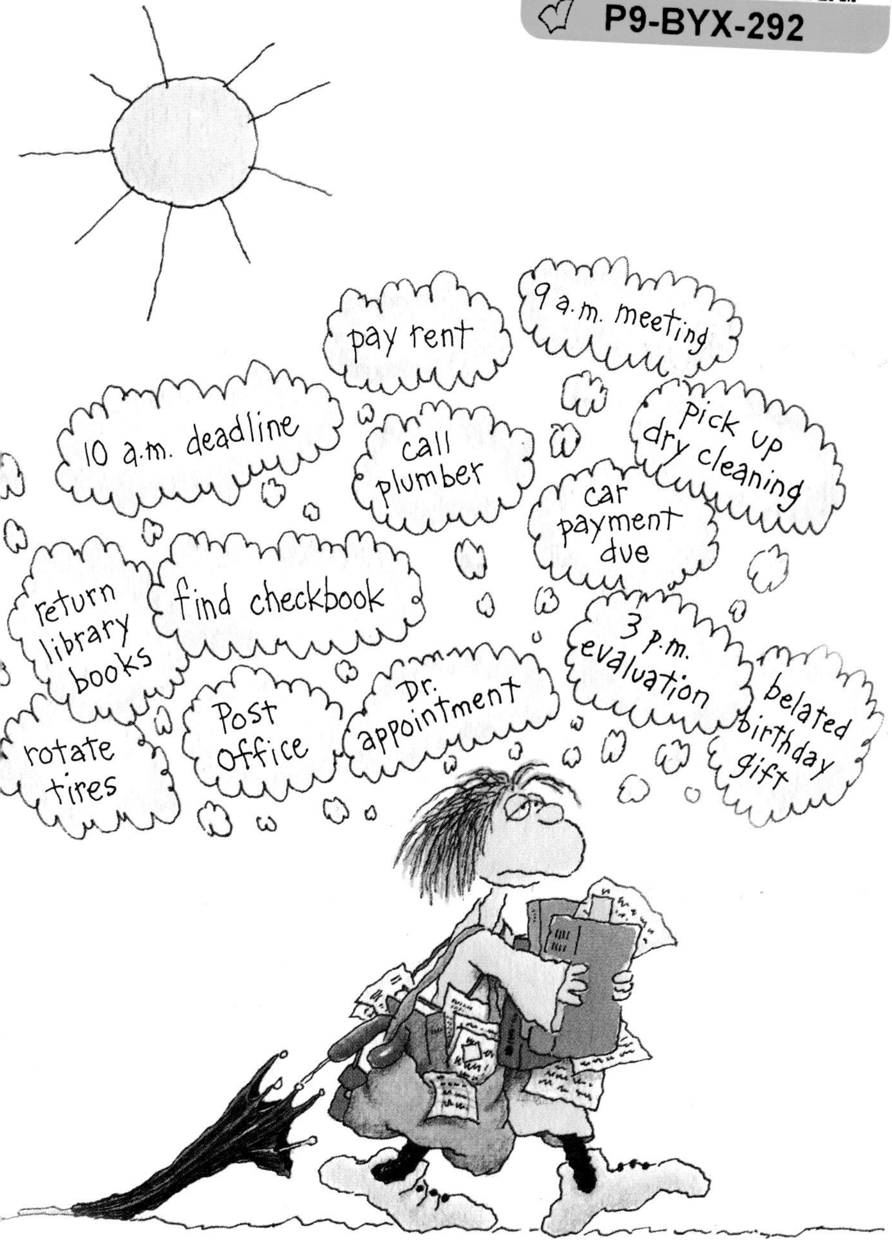
pay rent
9 a.m. meeting
10 a.m. deadline
call plumber
pick up dry cleaning
car payment due
return library books
find checkbook
3 p.m. evaluation
rotate tires
Post Office
Dr. appointment
belated birthday gift

64 WAYS TO BEAT THE BLUES

BY YOLANDA NAVE

WORKMAN PUBLISHING • NEW YORK

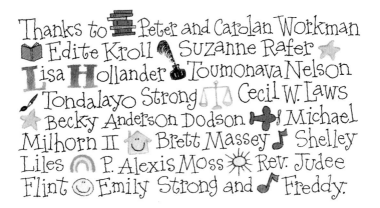

Thanks to Peter and Carolan Workman Edite Kroll Suzanne Rafer Lisa Hollander Toumonava Nelson Tondalayo Strong Cecil W. Laws Becky Anderson Dodson Michael Milhorn II Brett Massey Shelley Liles P. Alexis Moss Rev. Judee Flint Emily Strong and Freddy.

Published simultaneously in Canada by Thomas Allen and Son Limited.

Library of Congress Cataloging-in-Publication Data
Nave, Yolanda
64 ways to beat the blues / by Yolanda Nave.
p. cm.
ISBN 0-7611-0596-4
1. Humor. II. Title: Sixty-four ways to beat the blues. II. Title.
PN6231.D43 N38 1999
741.5'973—dc21 99-041385
CIP

Cover and book design by Lisa Hollander

Workman books are available at special discounts when purchased in bulk for premiums and sales promotions as well as for fund-raising or educational use. Special editions or book excerpts can be created to specification. For details, contact the Special Sales Director at the address below.

Workman Publishing Company, Inc.
708 Broadway
New York, NY 10003-9555

www.workmanweb.com

First printing October 1999

10 9 8 7 6 5 4 3 2 1

Dedicated to those who...
pushed my buttons, rocked my boat,
burst my bubble, darkened my door,
ran me ragged, rained on my parade, or
dampened my spirits
and sent me a bill.

AM I BLUE?

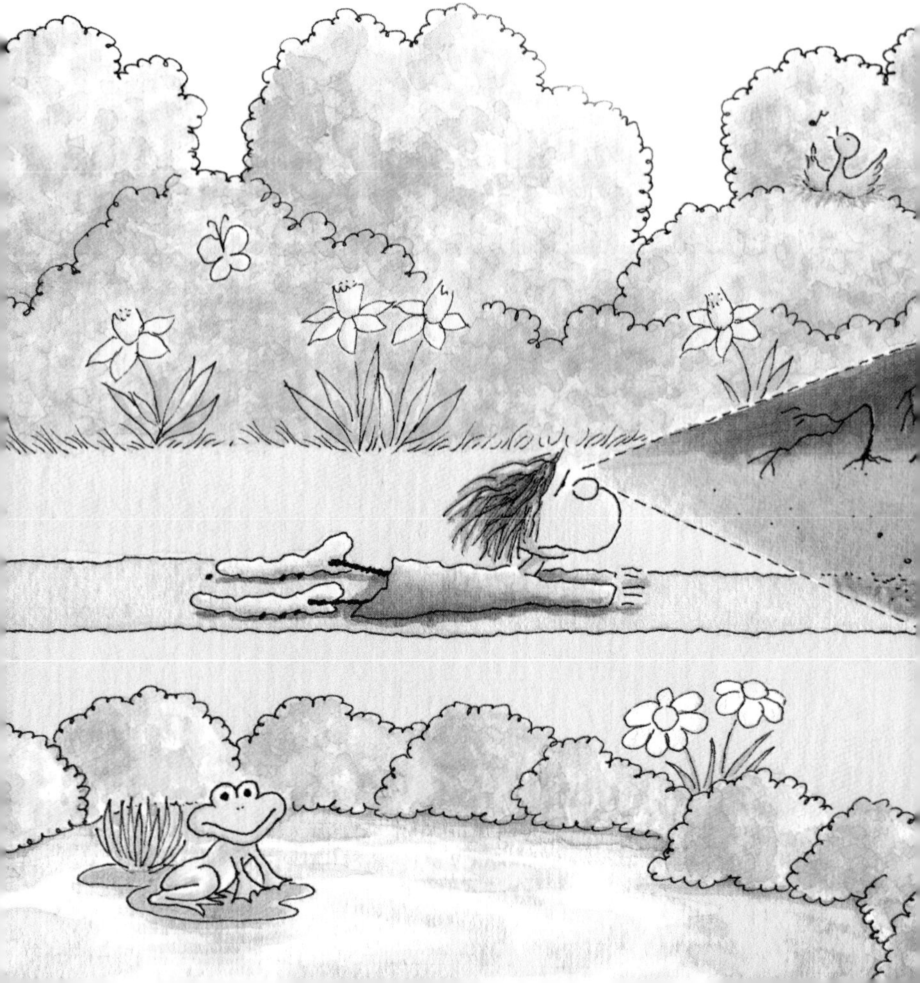

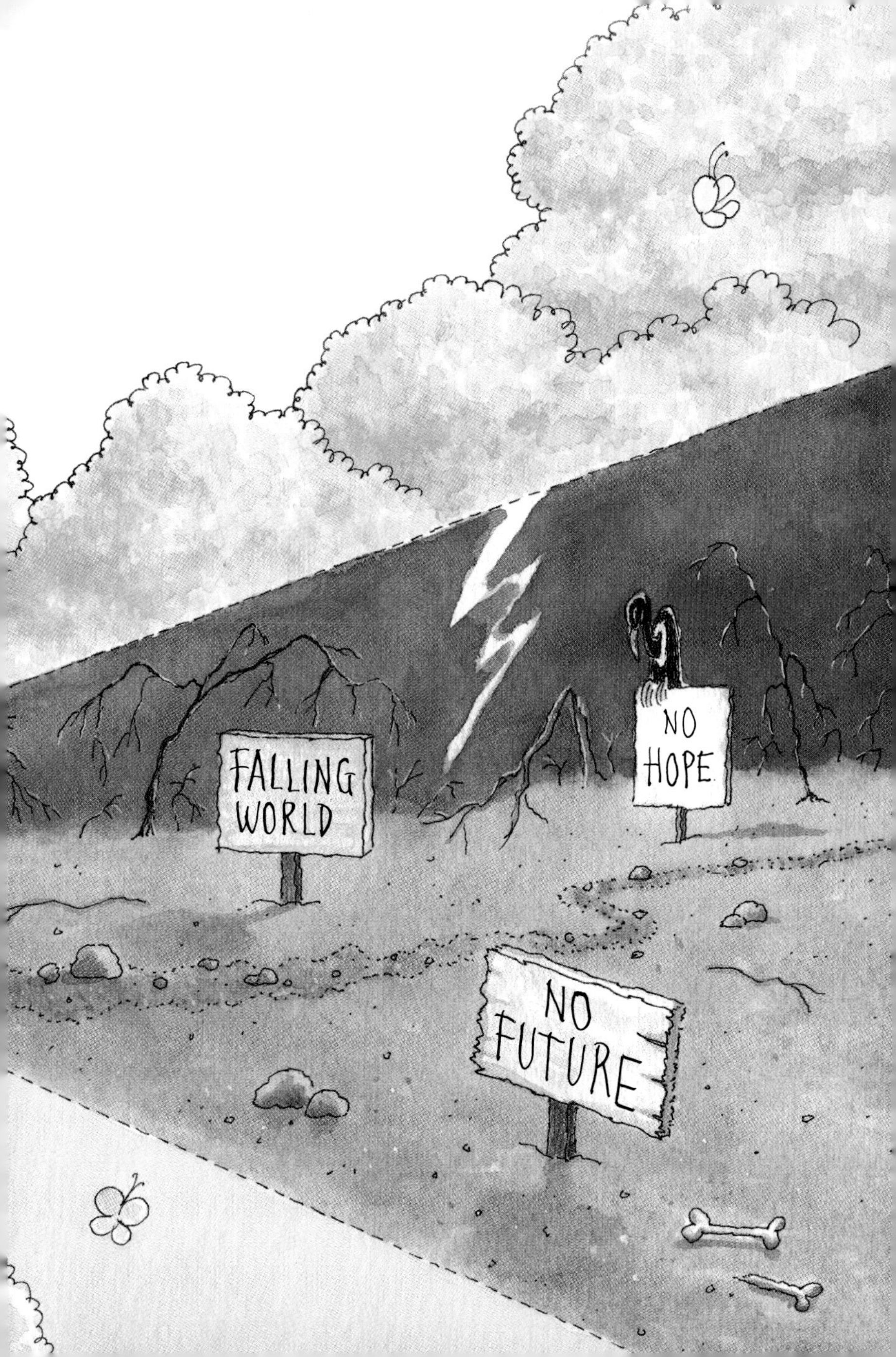
FALLING WORLD
NO HOPE
NO FUTURE

Almost everyone gets the blues now and then.

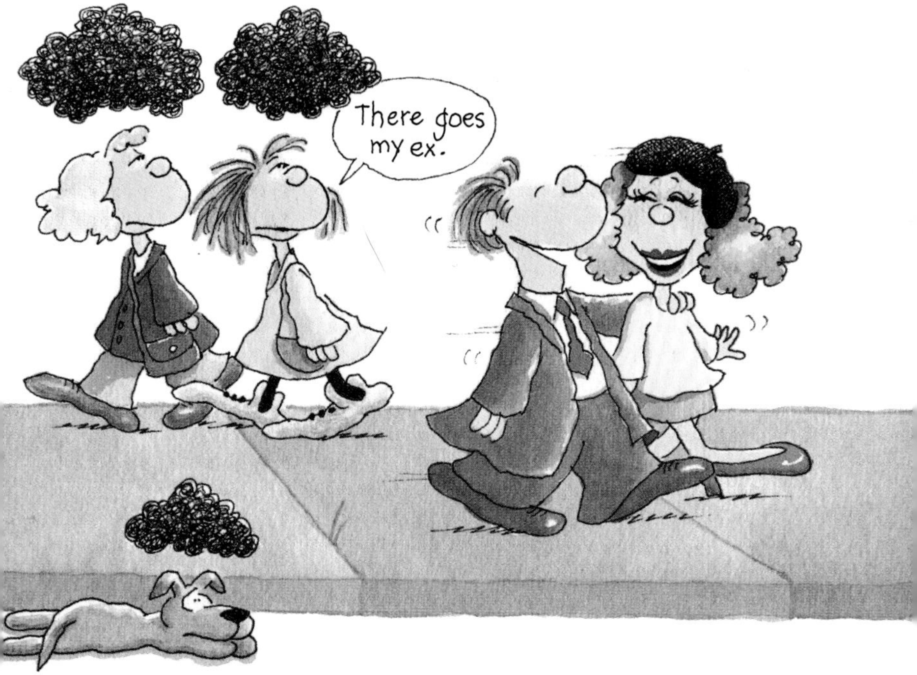
There goes my ex.

Blues can range from mild...

to moderate...

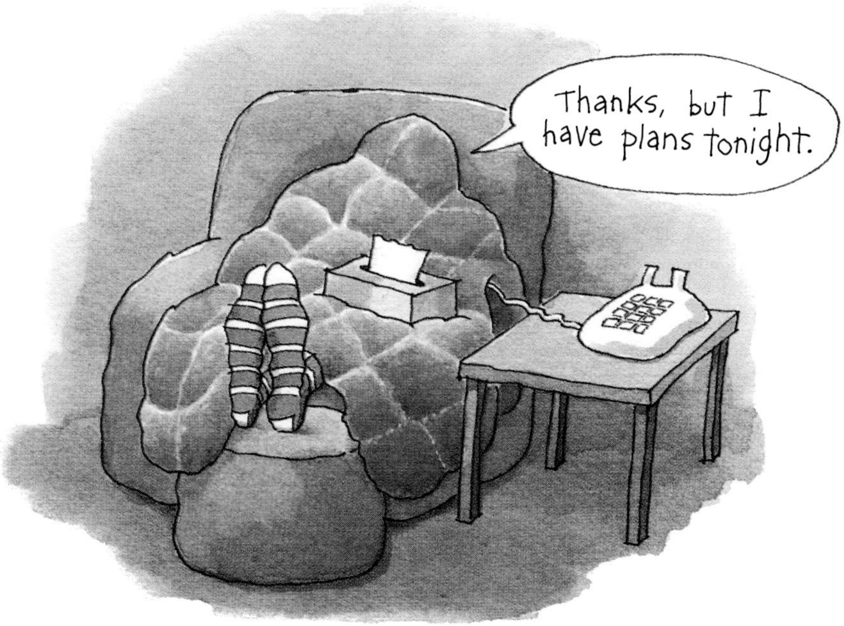
Thanks, but I have plans tonight.

to comatose.

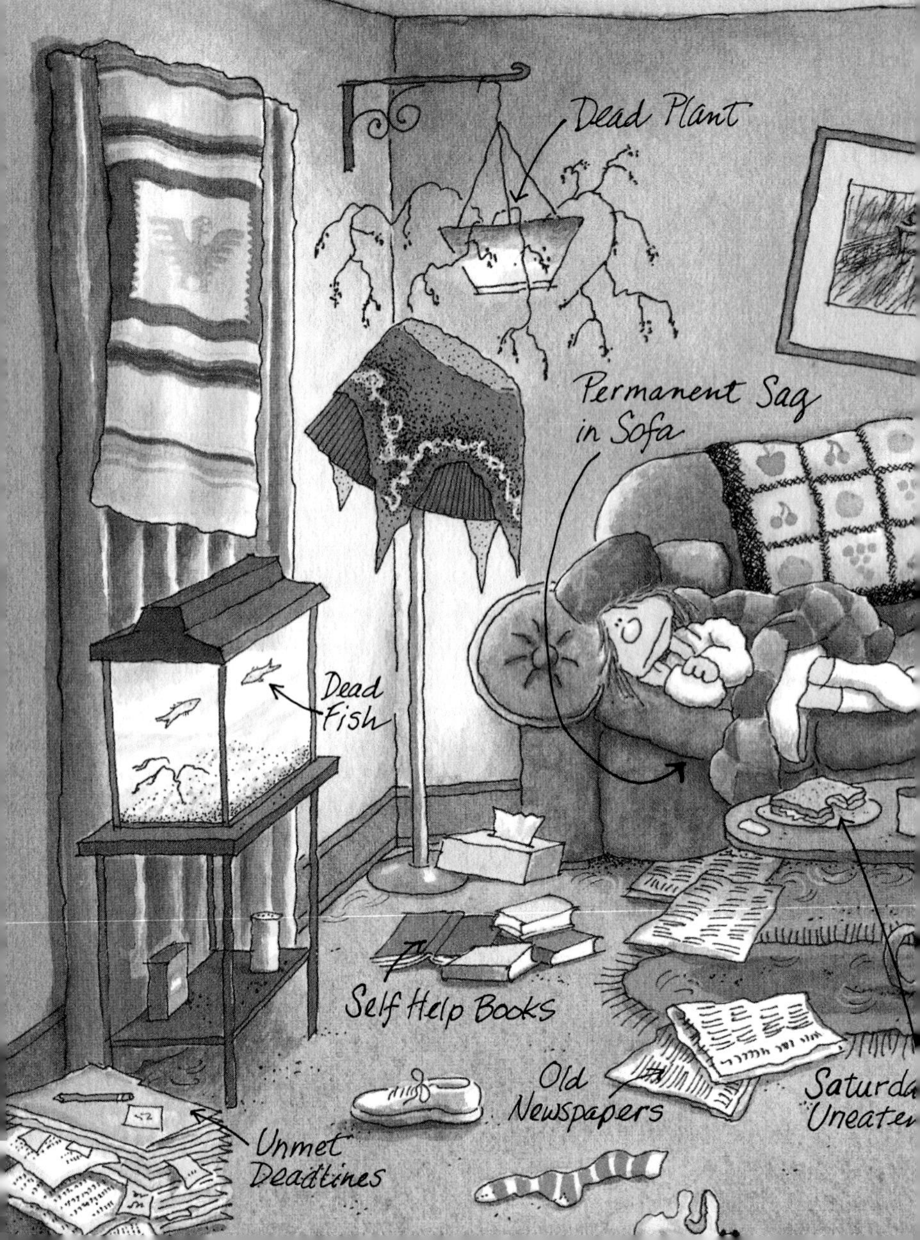
Dead Plant
Permanent Sag in Sofa
Dead Fish
Self Help Books
Old Newspapers
Saturda
Uneaten
Unmet Deadlines

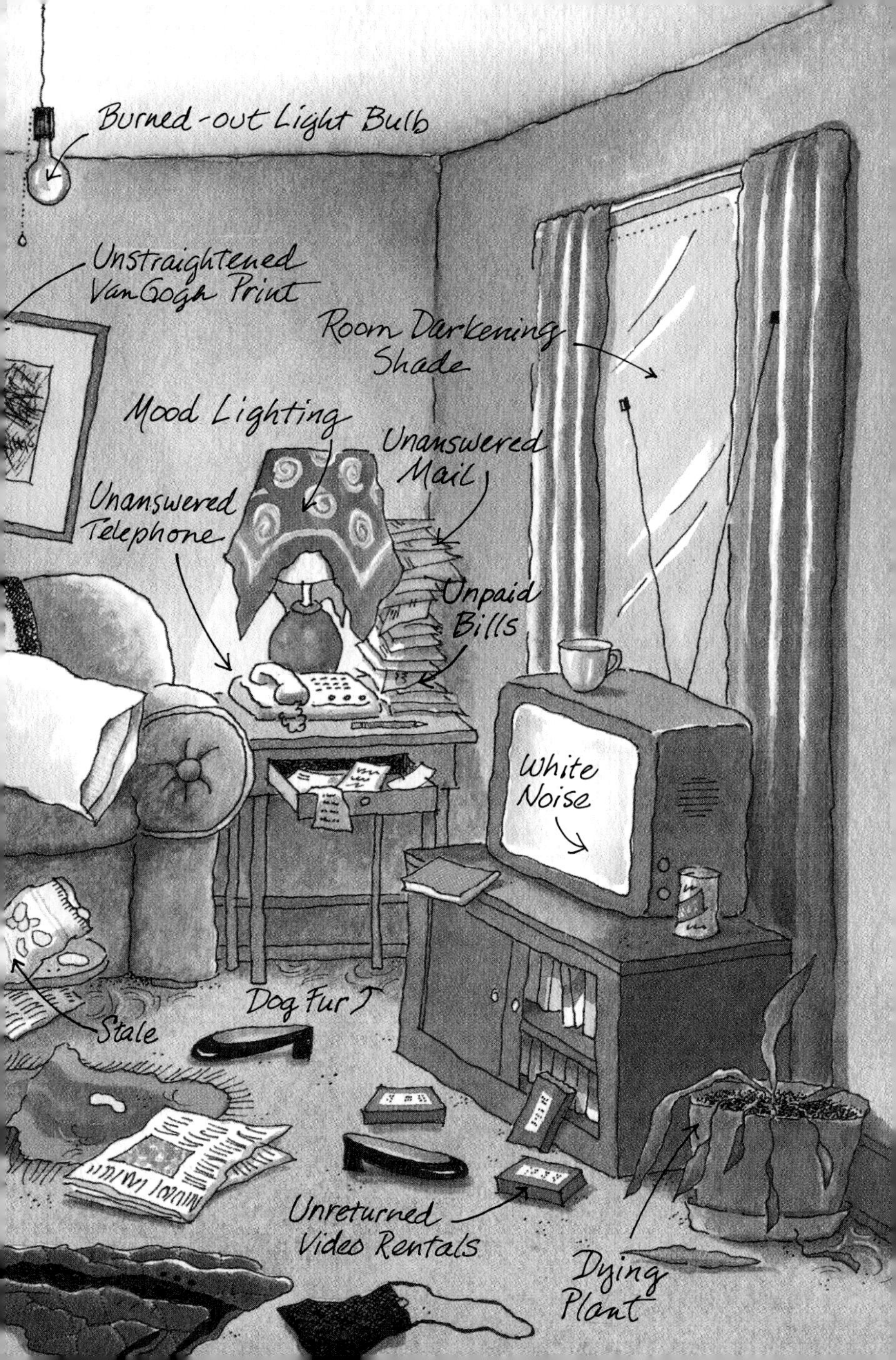
Burned-out Light Bulb
Unstraightened Van Gogh Print
Room Darkening Shade
Mood Lighting
Unanswered Mail
Unanswered Telephone
Unpaid Bills
White Noise
Dog Fur
Stale
Unreturned Video Rentals
Dying Plant

They may be seasonal...

occupational...

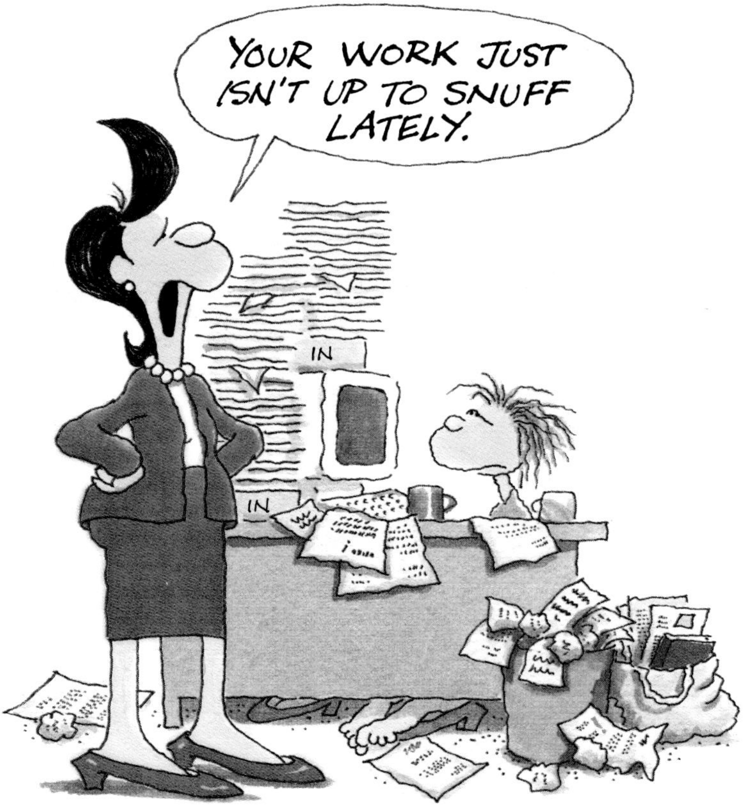
YOUR WORK JUST ISN'T UP TO SNUFF LATELY.
IN
IN

hormonal...

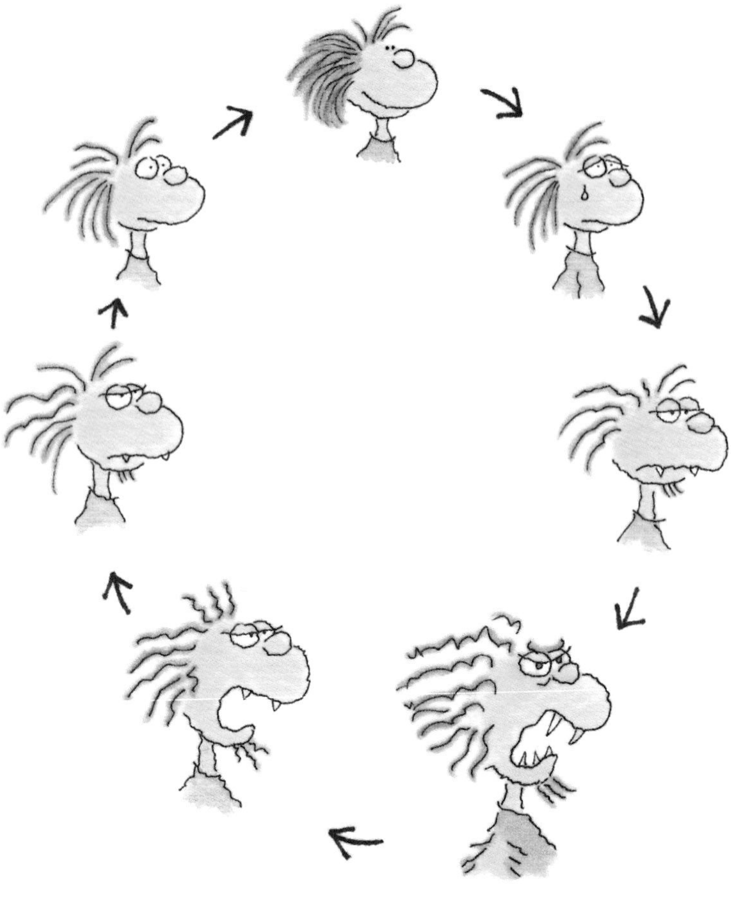

or matrimonial.

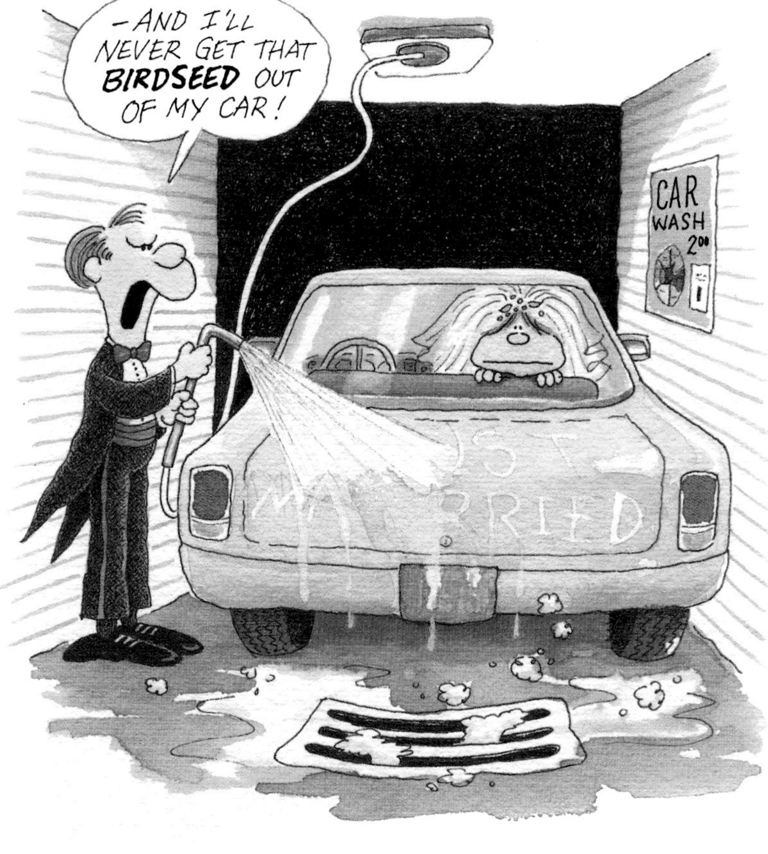
–AND I'LL NEVER GET THAT BIRDSEED OUT OF MY CAR!
CAR WASH 2.00
JUST MARRIED

Whether you've inherited your blues...

or acquired them one by one...

it's time for a change.

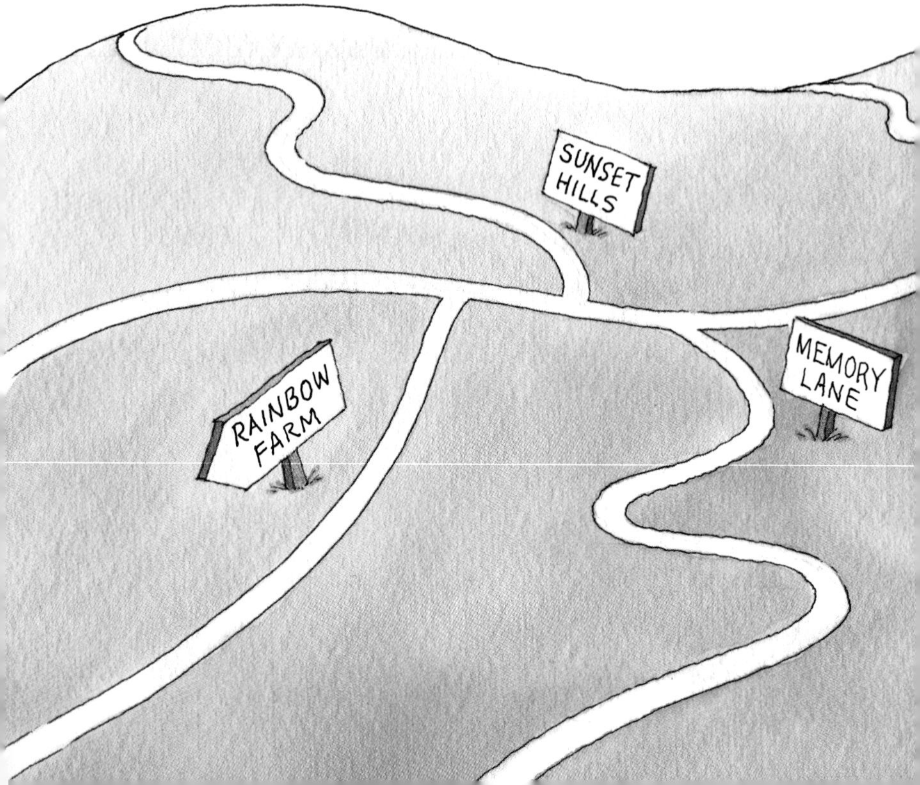
SUNSET
HILLS
MEMORY
LANE
RAINBOW
FARM

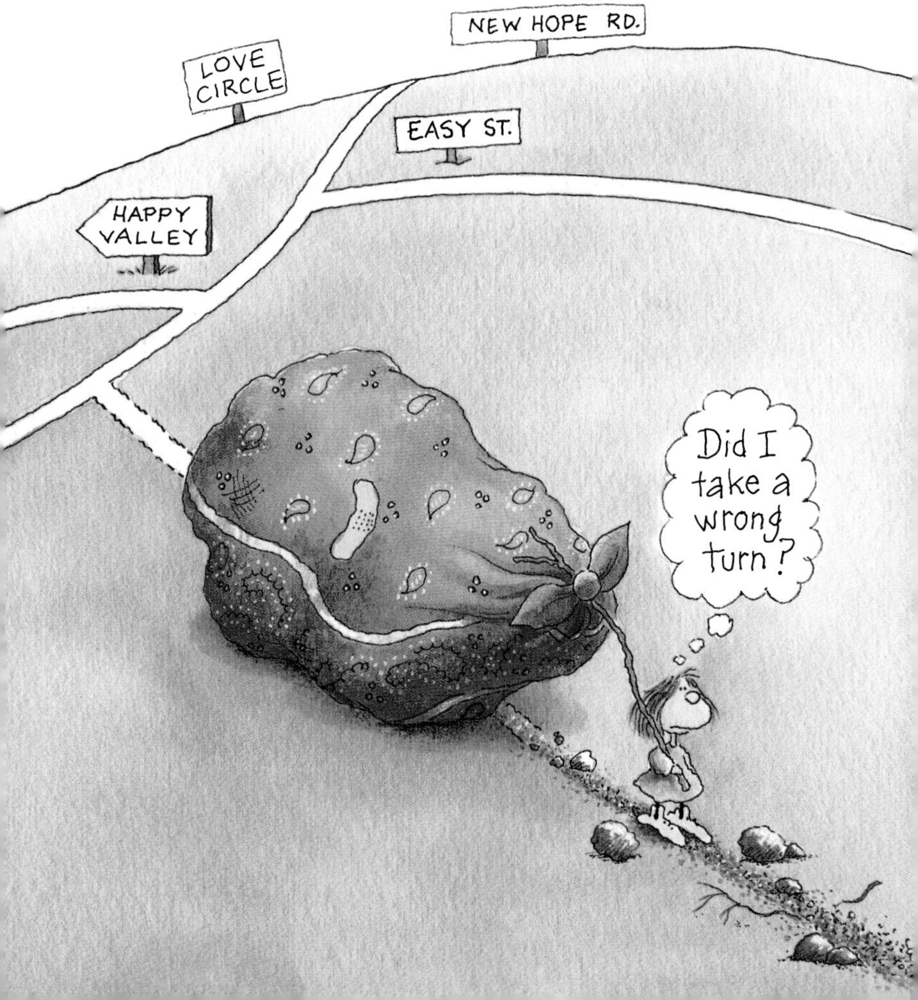
NEW HOPE RD.
LOVE CIRCLE
EASY ST.
HAPPY VALLEY
Did I take a wrong turn?

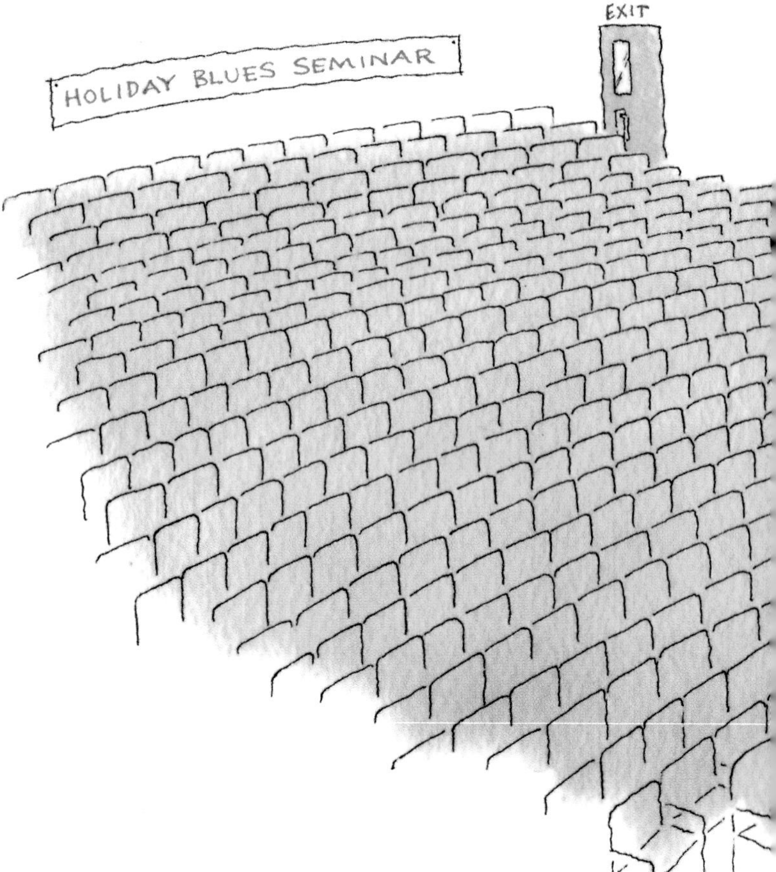
EXIT
HOLIDAY BLUES SEMINAR

BEAT THE BLUES

We'll wait another 15 minutes.

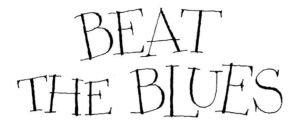

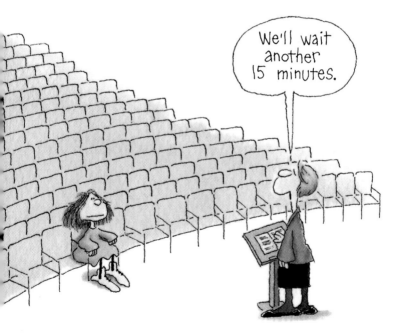

1

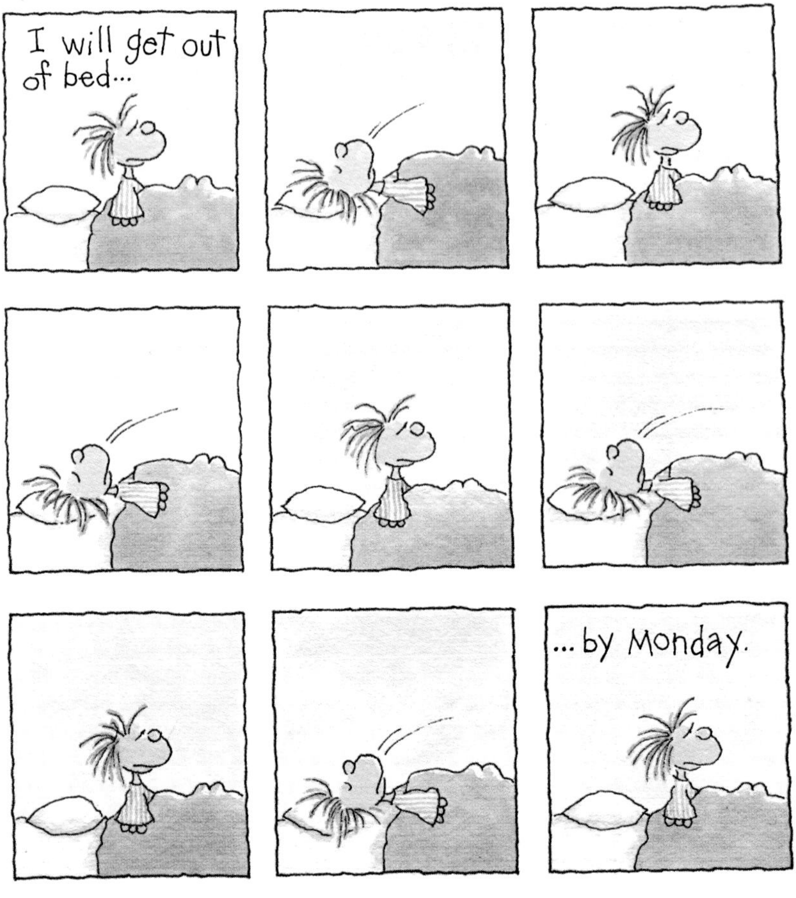
I will get out of bed...
... by Monday.

Set small goals.

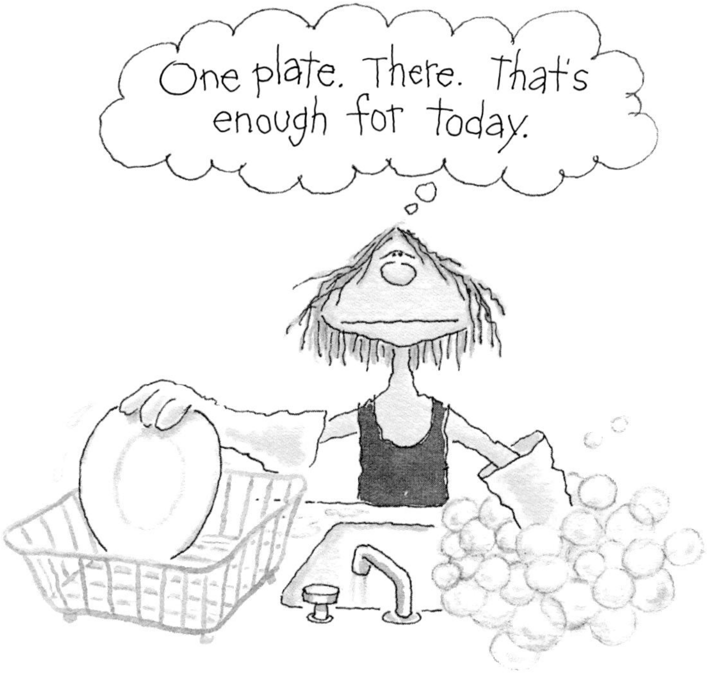
One plate. There. That's enough for today.

2 Take antidepressants.

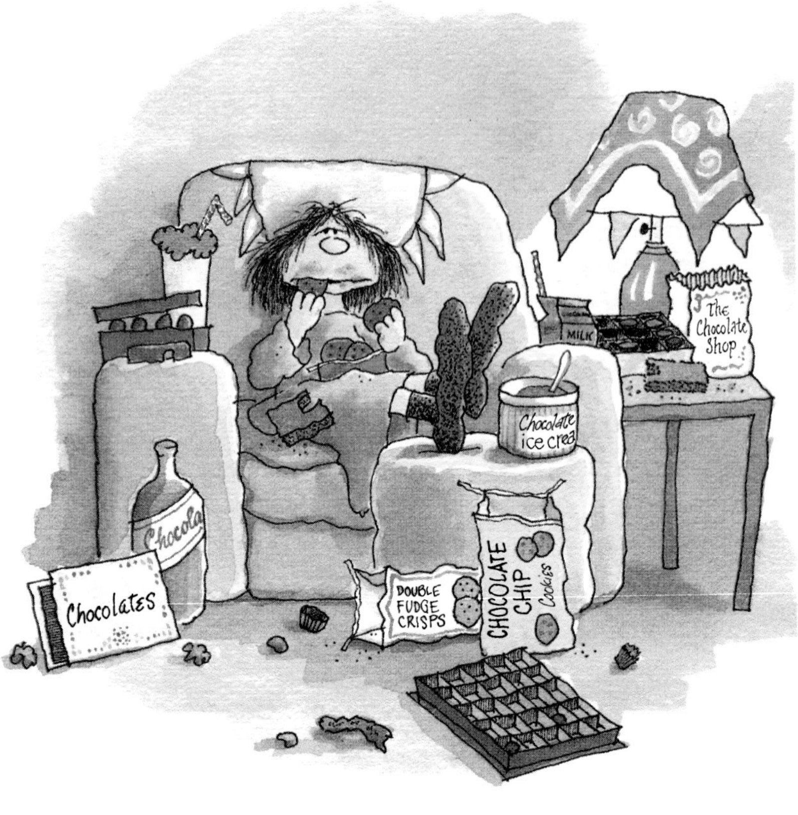
The Chocolate Shop
MILK
Chocolate ice crea
Chocola
Chocolates
DOUBLE FUDGE CRISPS
CHOCOLATE CHIP Cookies

Get some exercise.

4

Rule out a vitamin deficiency.

5 Get a checkup.

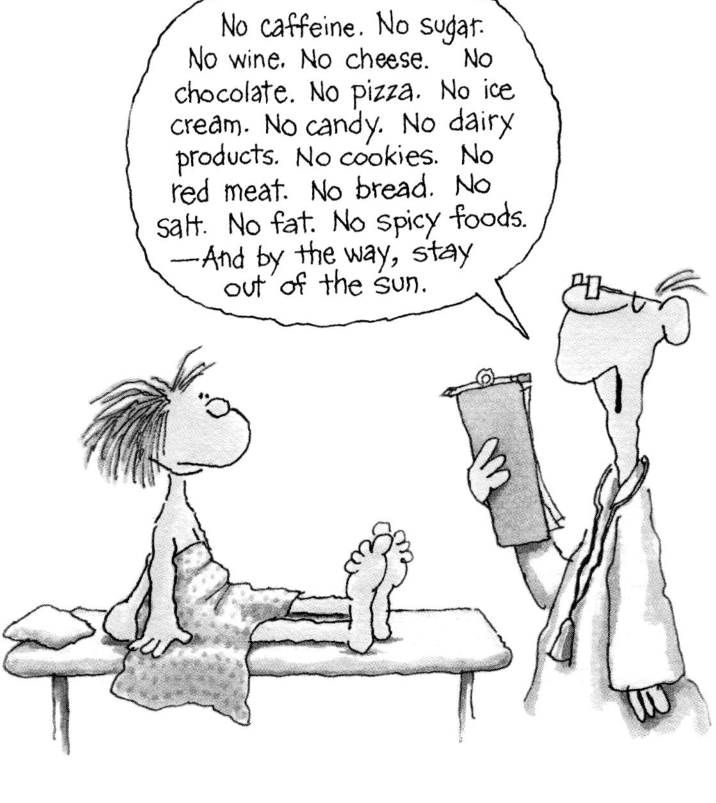
No caffeine. No sugar. No wine. No cheese. No chocolate. No pizza. No ice cream. No candy. No dairy products. No cookies. No red meat. No bread. No salt. No fat. No spicy foods. —And by the way, stay out of the sun.

6

Find a change of scenery.

7

Get a pet.

8 Try shopping.

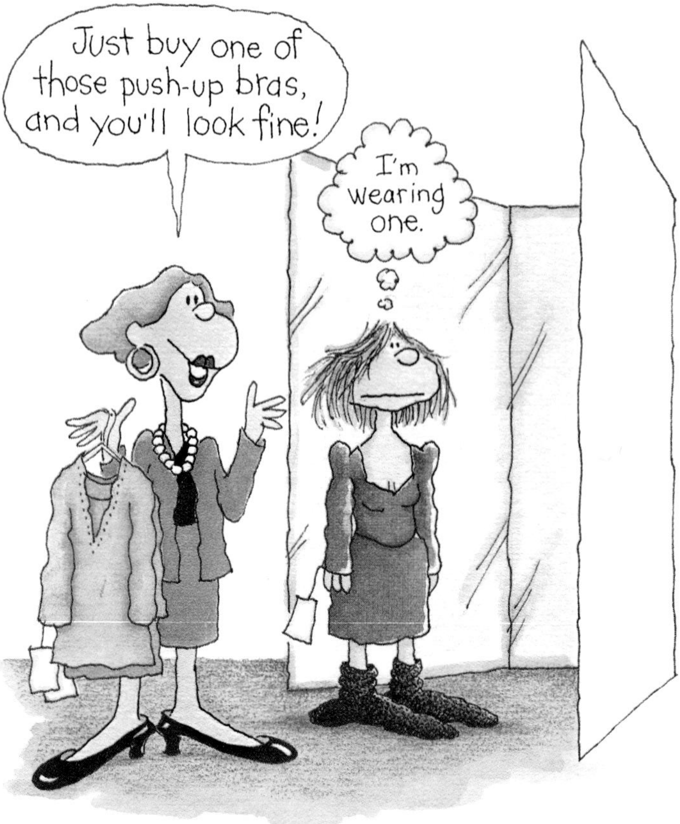
Just buy one of those push-up bras, and you'll look fine!
I'm wearing one.

Take in a funny movie.

10

Practice affirmations.

11

Get a good night's sleep.

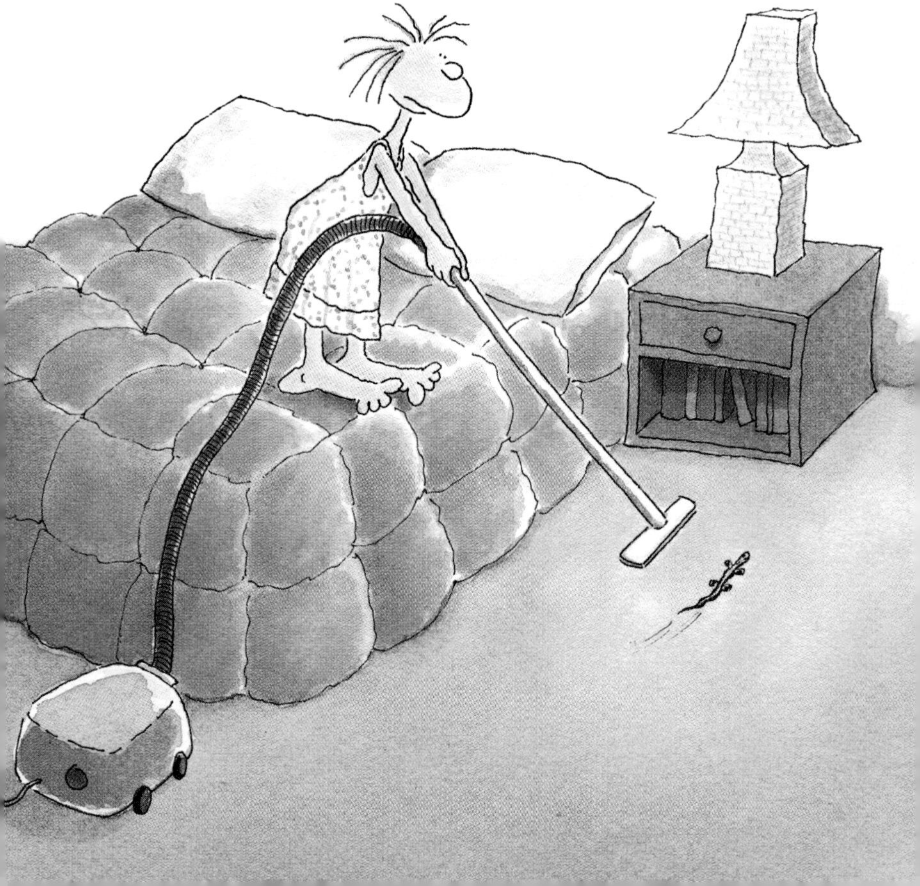

12 Who cares?

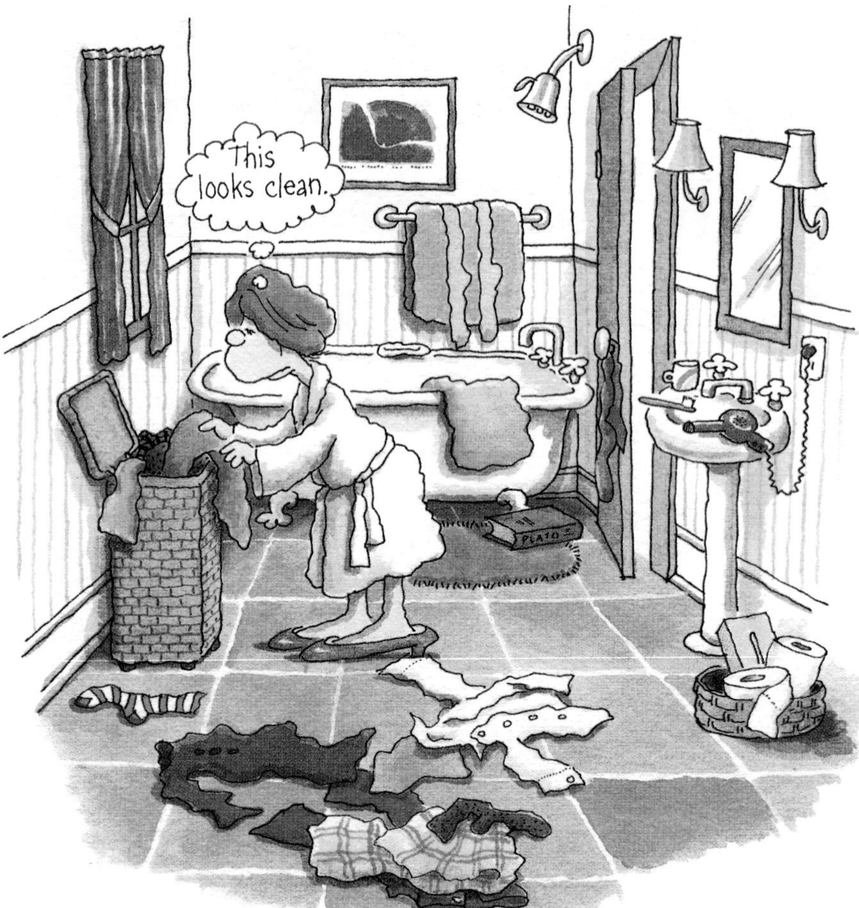
This looks clean.
PLATO

Lay in supplies for the winter.

14 Phone a friend.

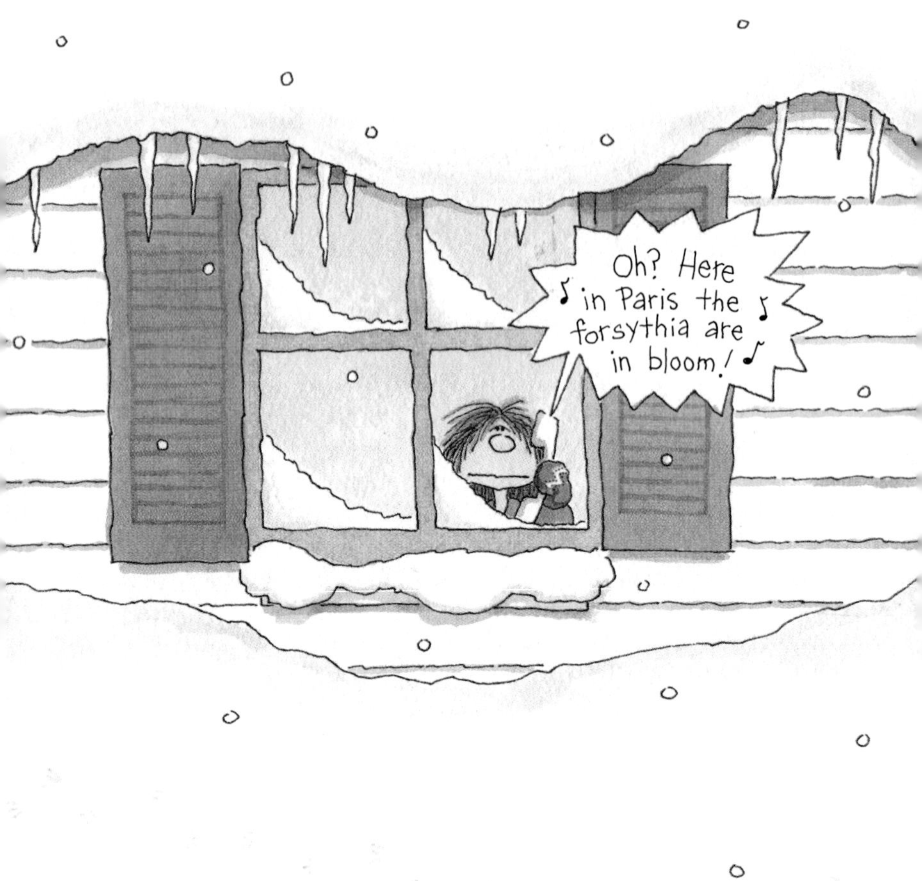
Oh? Here in Paris the forsythia are in bloom!

Try light therapy.

16 Go out to dinner.

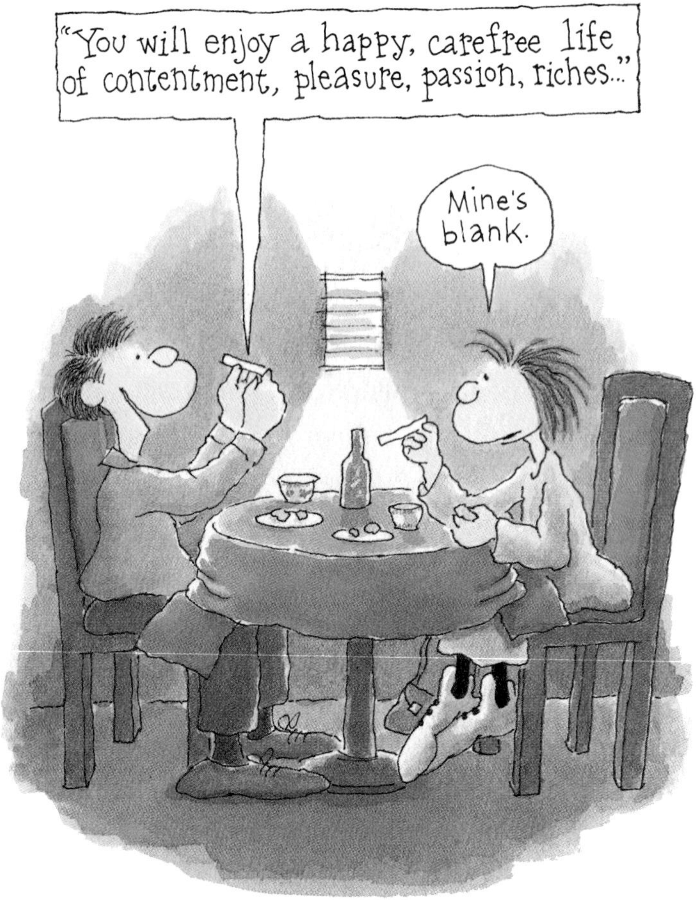
"You will enjoy a happy, carefree life of contentment, pleasure, passion, riches..."
Mine's blank.

17 Read a good book.

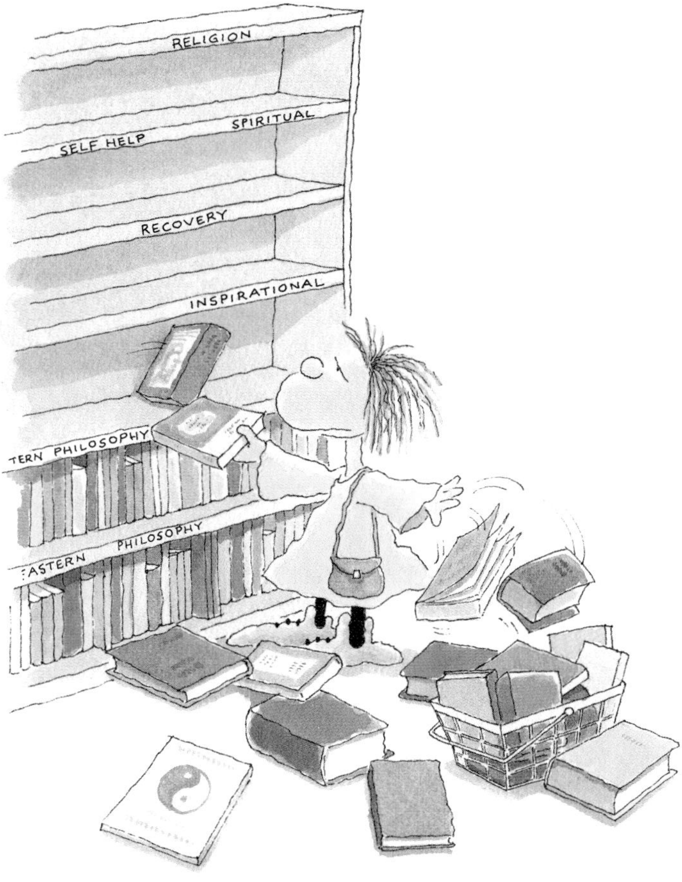
RELIGION
SPIRITUAL
SELF HELP
RECOVERY
INSPIRATIONAL
TERN PHILOSOPHY
EASTERN PHILOSOPHY

18

Research your genealogy.

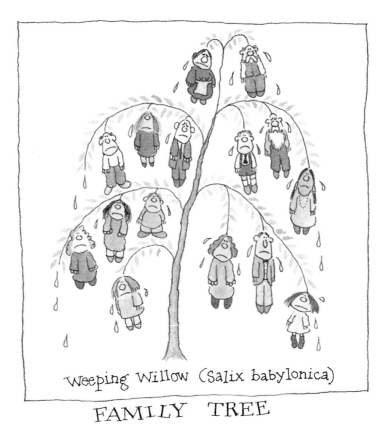

Weeping Willow (Salix babylonica)

FAMILY TREE

19

Claim your inheritance!

20 Find a good shrink.

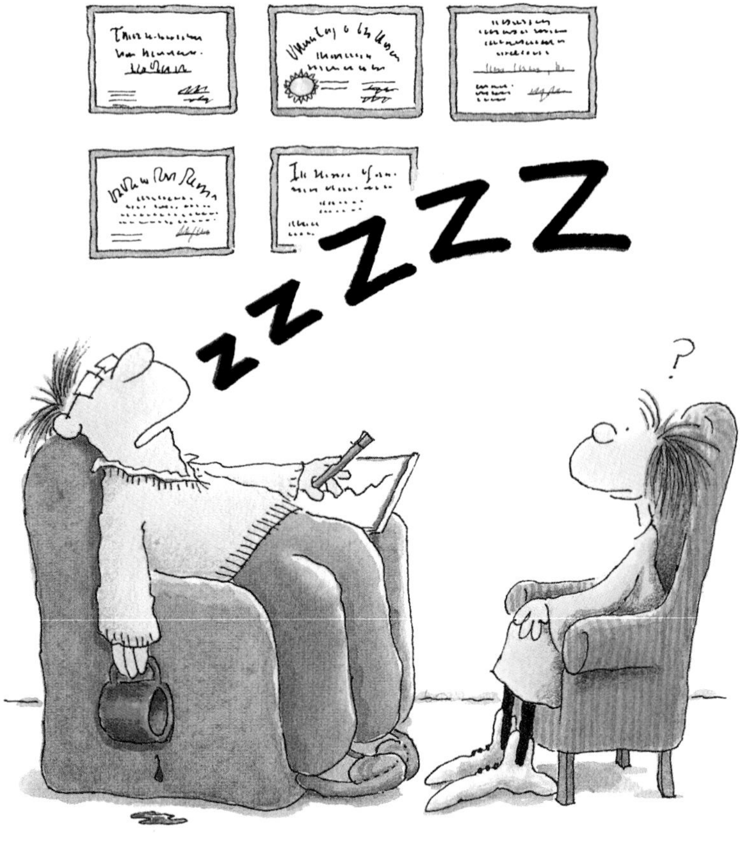
ZZZZZZ
?

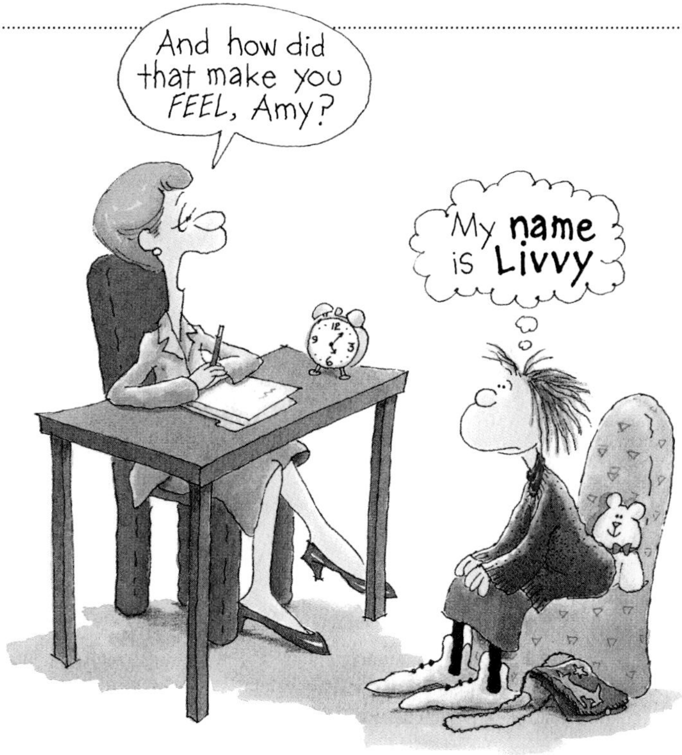
And how did that make you FEEL, Amy?
My name is Livvy

21

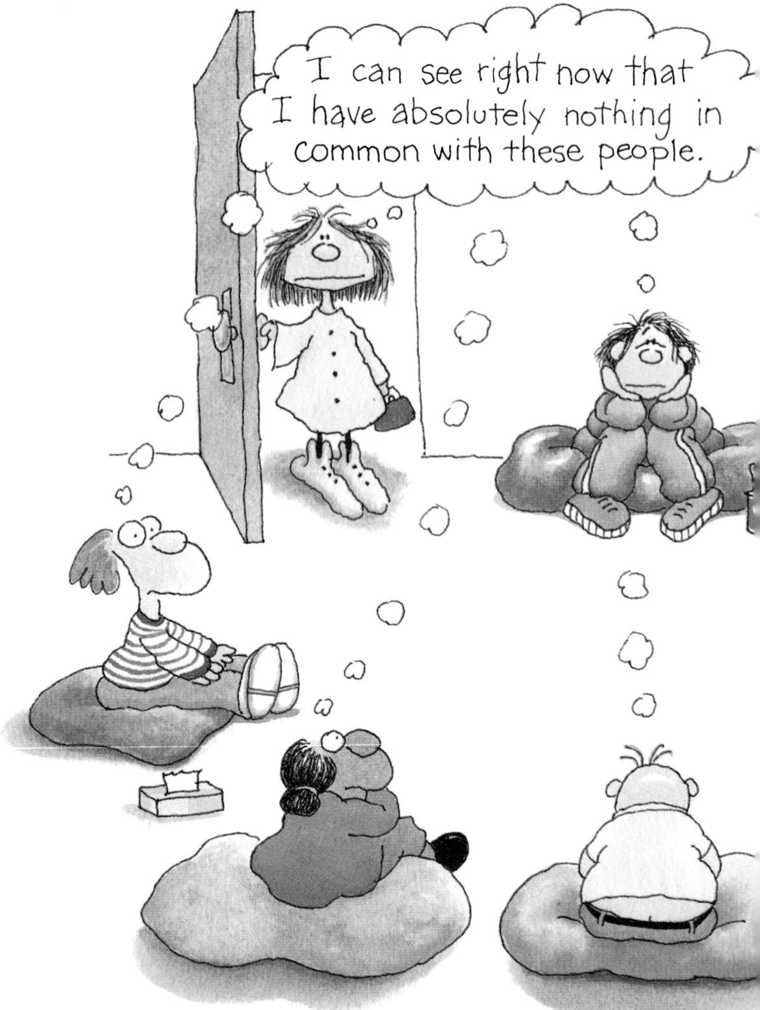
I can see right now that
I have absolutely nothing in
common with these people.

Join a group.

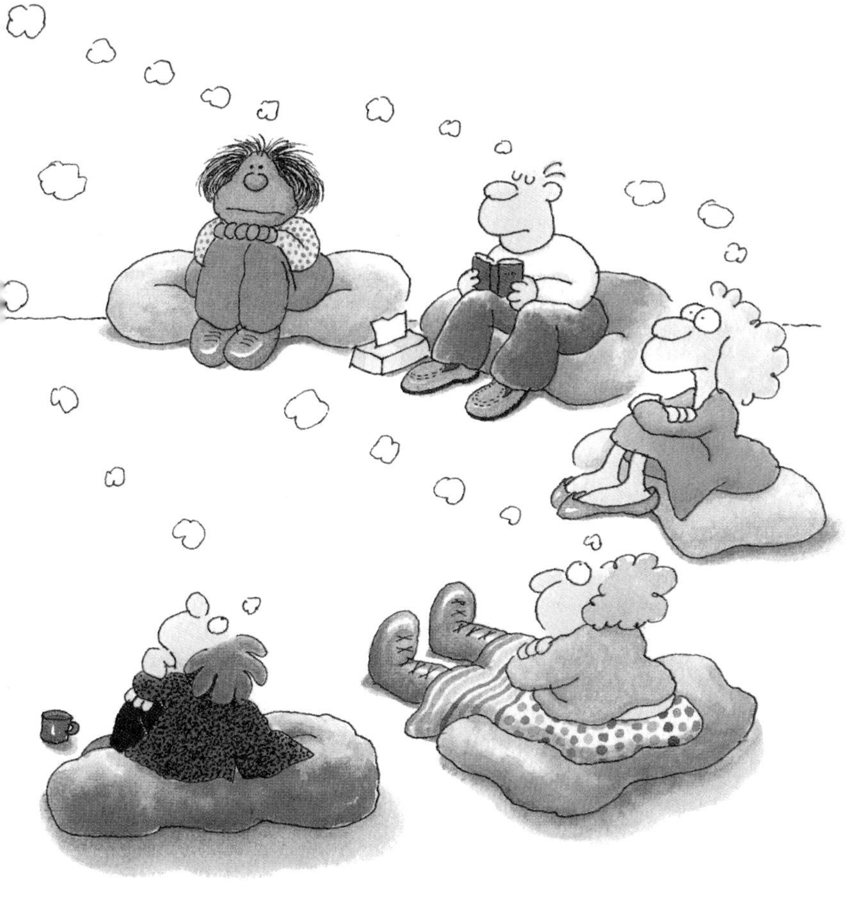

22 Keep a journal.

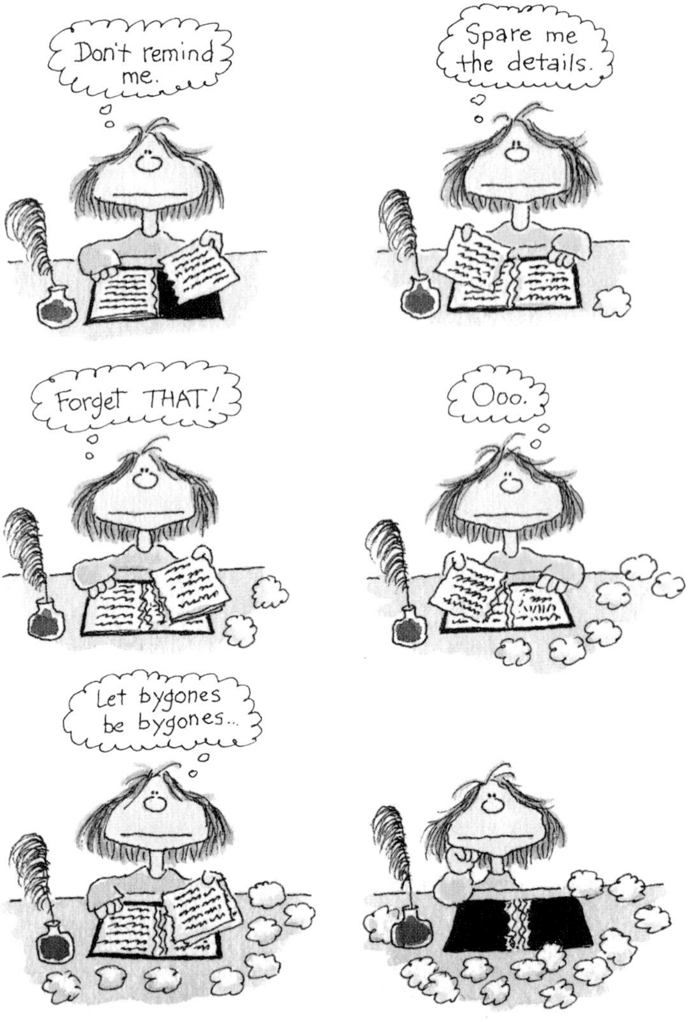
Don't remind me.
Spare me the details.
Forget THAT!
Ooo.
Let bygones be bygones...

23 Ask for help.

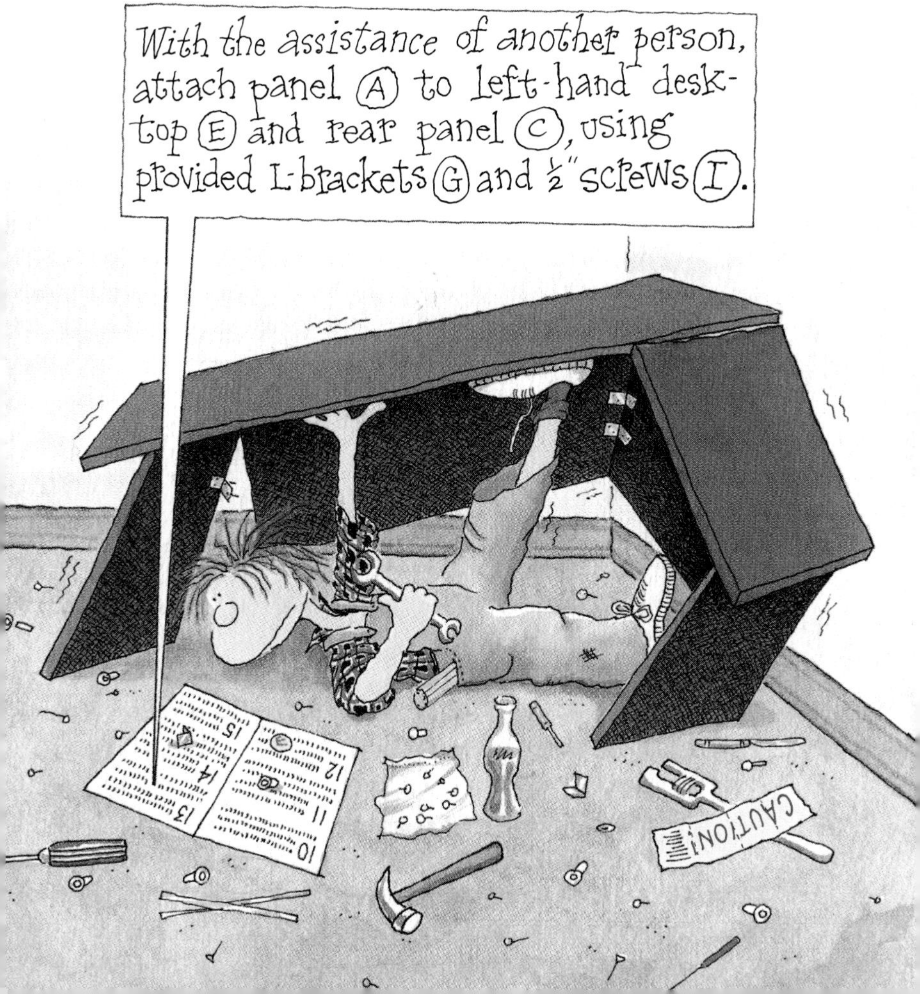
With the assistance of another person, attach panel (A) to left-hand desk-top (E) and rear panel (C), using provided L-brackets (G) and ½" screws (I).
CAUTION!

24 Go easy on yourself.

HAIR SPRAY
ALL PURPOSE WOOD GLUE
HAIR CREAM
HAIR STYLING FOAM
SPRAY ADHESIVE
MOUSSE
HAIR MIST
STYLING GEL

Don't take it personally.

26 Say what you mean.

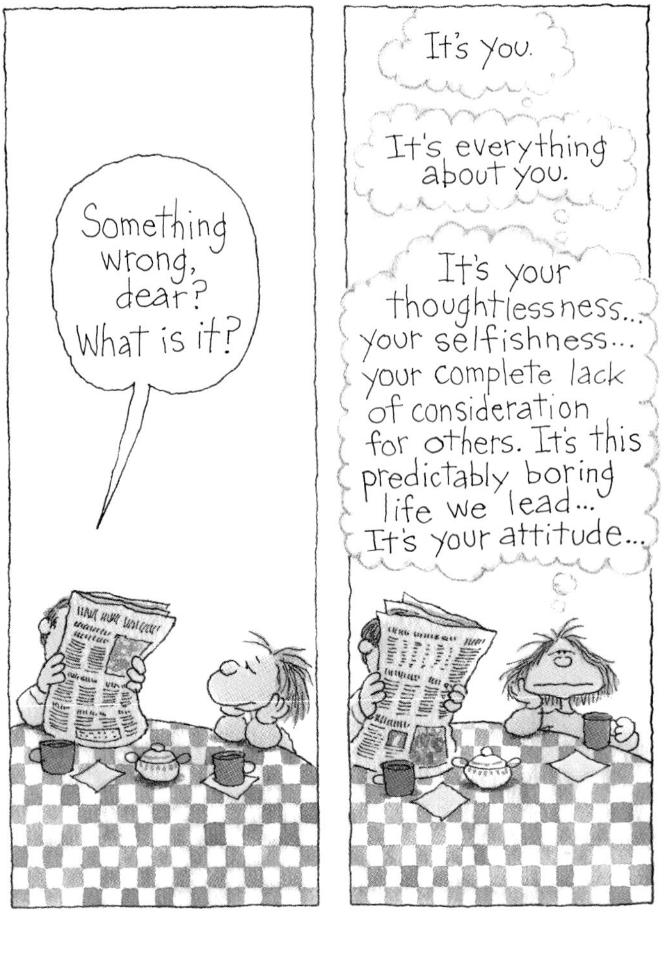
Something wrong, dear? What is it?
It's you.
It's everything about you.
It's your thoughtlessness... your selfishness... your complete lack of consideration for others. It's this predictably boring life we lead... It's your attitude...

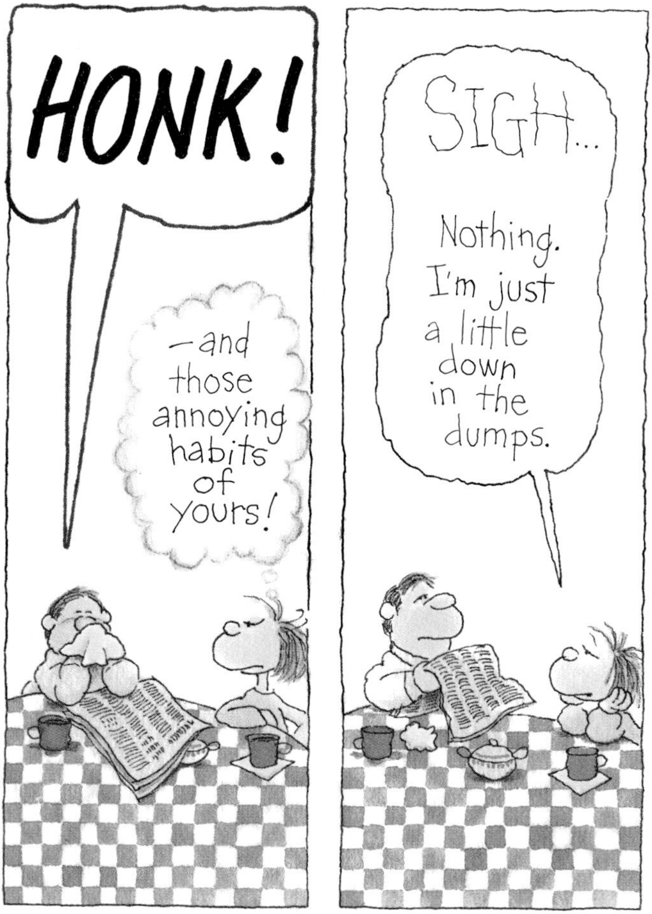
HONK!
—and those annoying habits of yours!
SIGH...
Nothing. I'm just a little down in the dumps.

27

Save major decisions for later.

28 Hire a good lawyer.

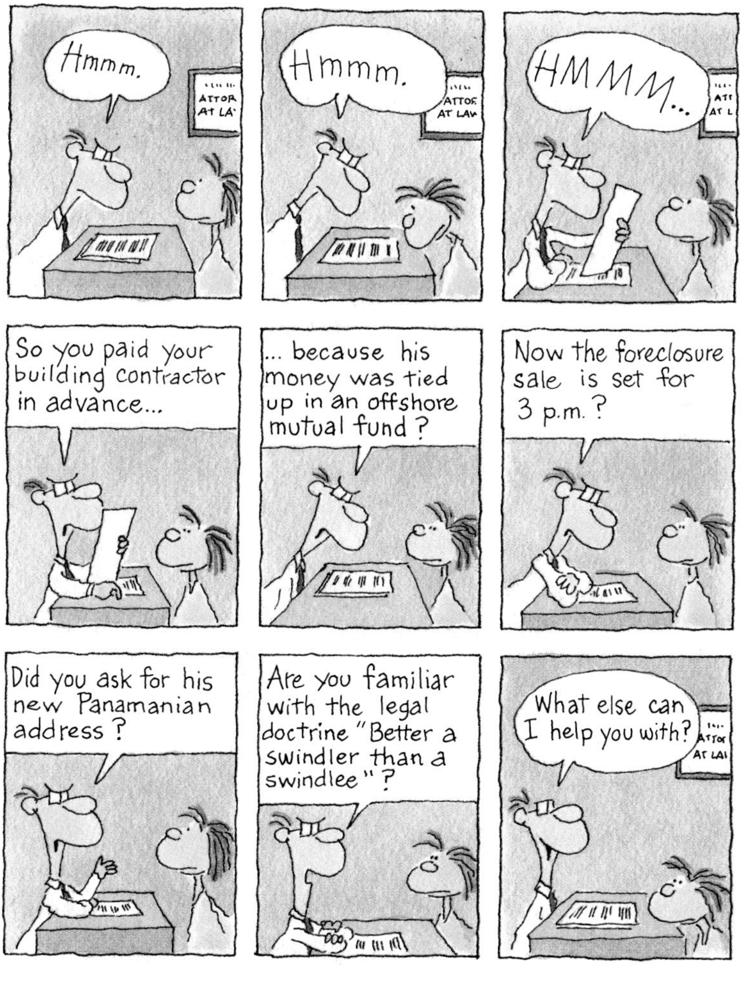
Hmmm.
ATTOR AT LA
Hmmm.
ATTOR AT LAW
HMMM...
So you paid your building contractor in advance...
... because his money was tied up in an offshore mutual fund?
Now the foreclosure sale is set for 3 p.m.?
Did you ask for his new Panamanian address?
Are you familiar with the legal doctrine "Better a swindler than a swindlee"?
What else can I help you with?
ATTOR AT LA

29

Be careful what you wish for.

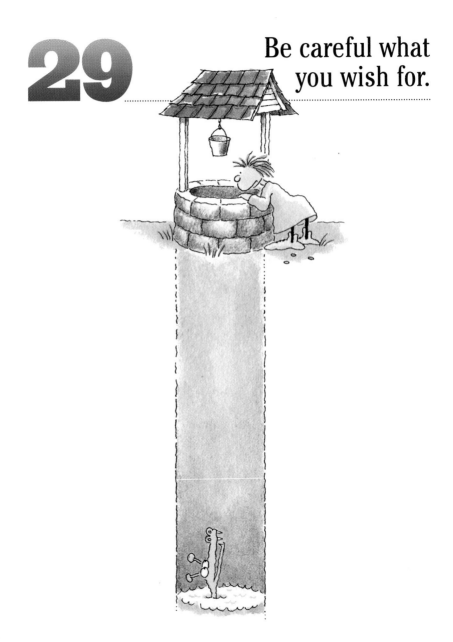

30

Test the waters.

31 Don't hold things inside.

32 Weed your garden.

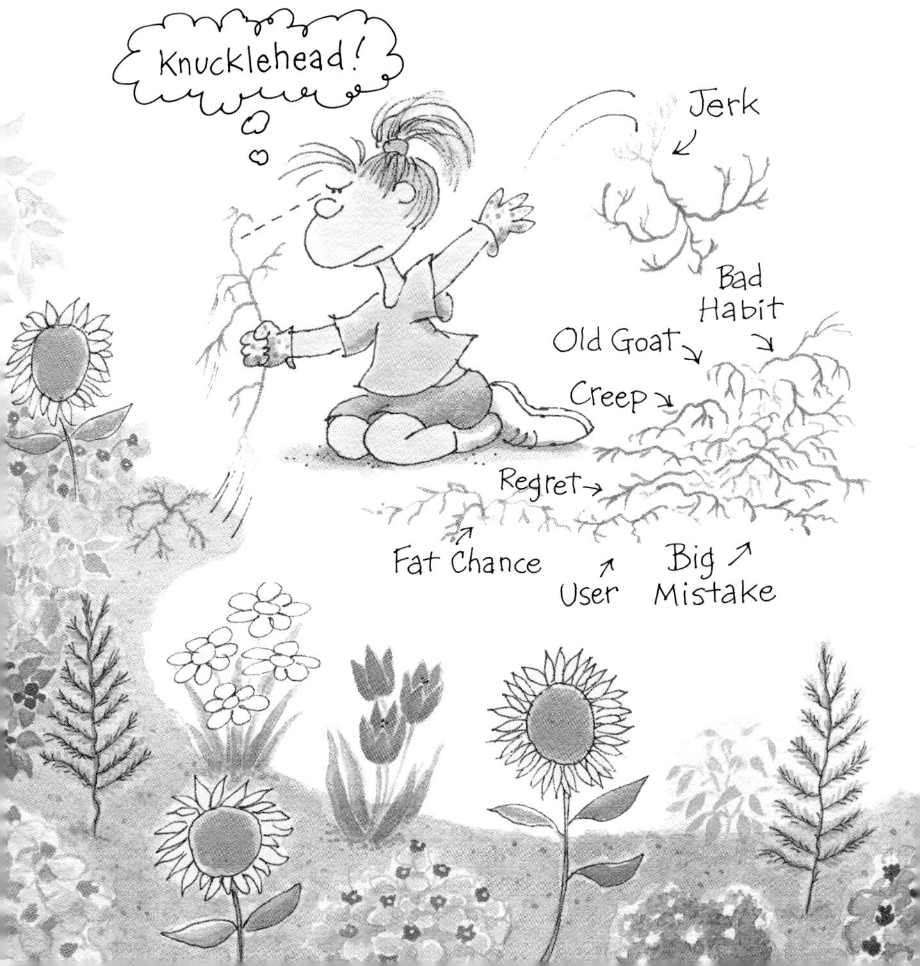
Knucklehead!
Jerk
Bad Habit
Old Goat
Creep
Regret
Fat Chance
User
Big Mistake

33 Rent a canoe.

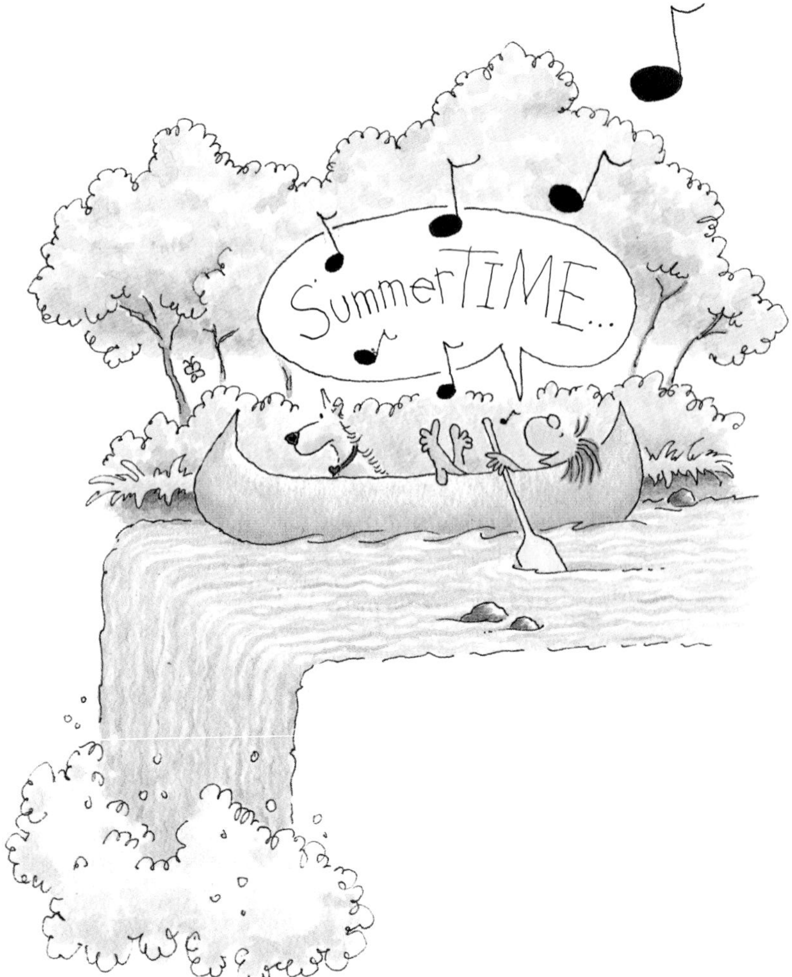
SummerTIME...

34 Take a helicopter ride!

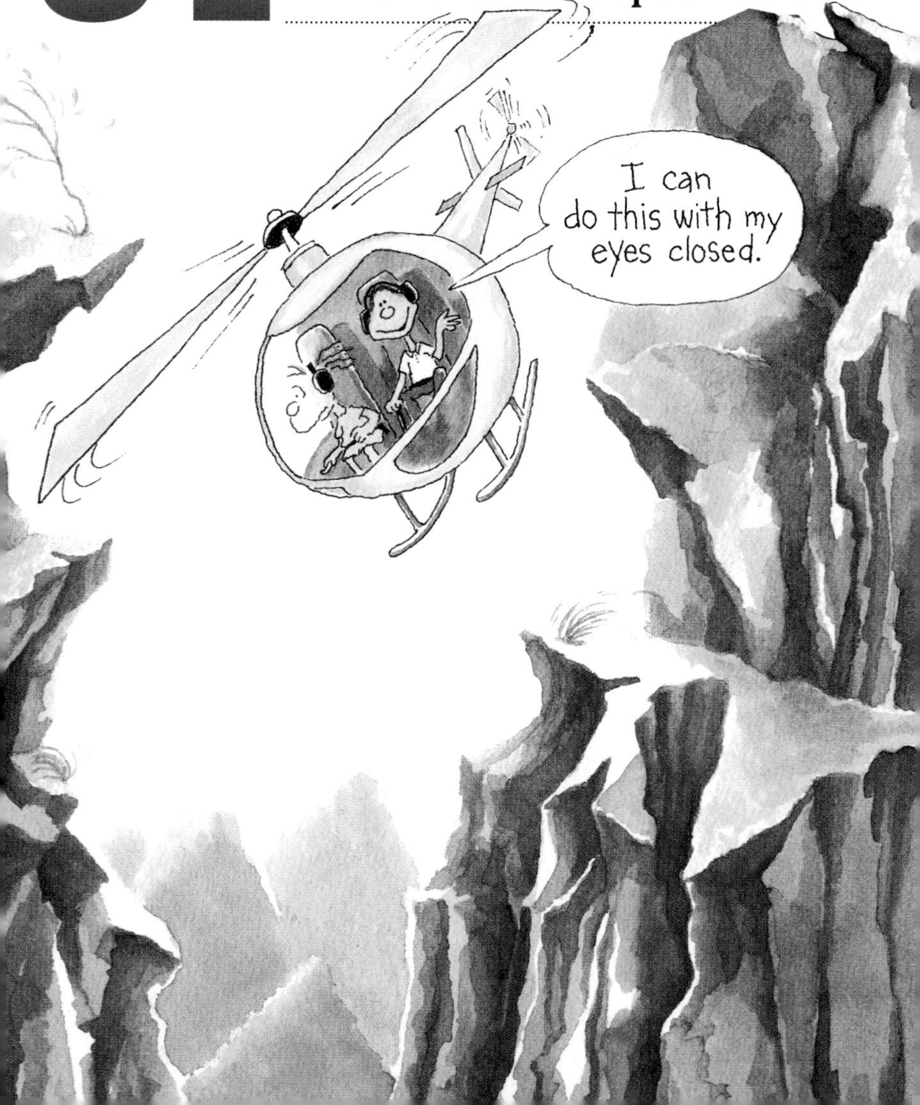
I can do this with my eyes closed.

35 Learn patience.

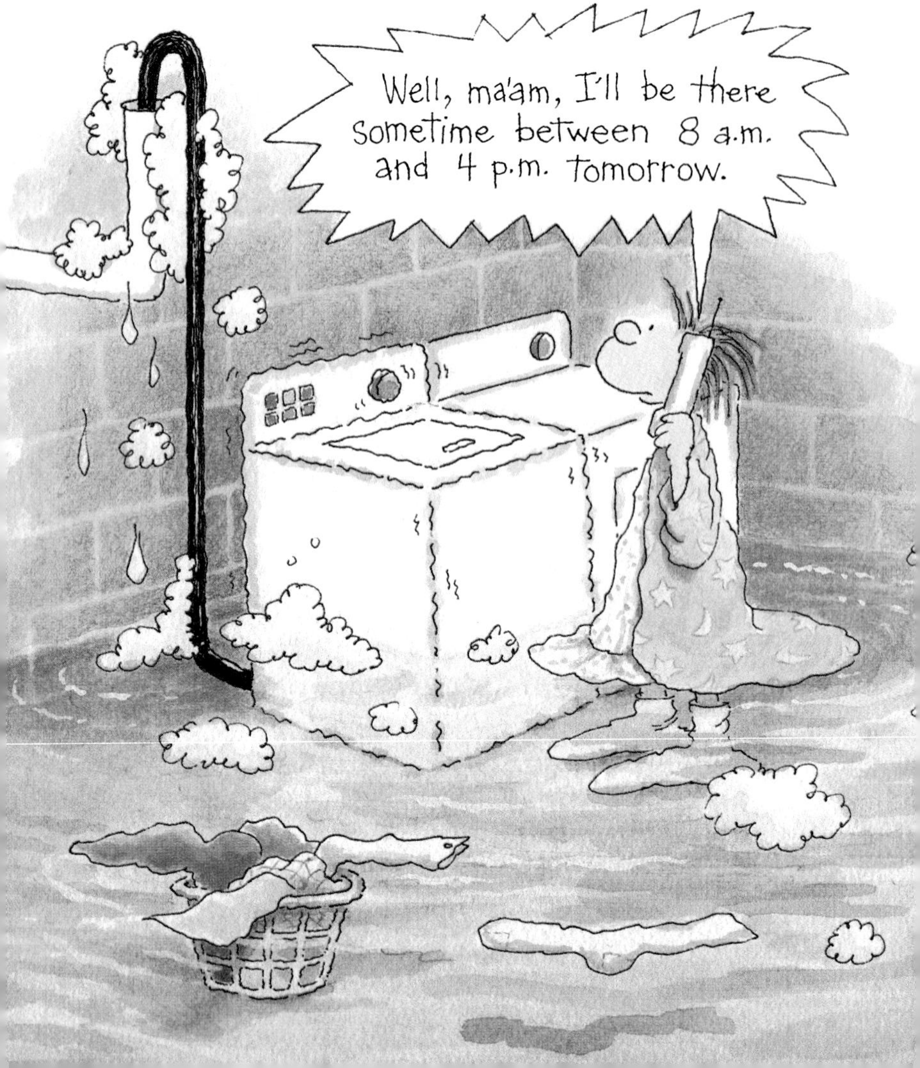
Well, ma'am, I'll be there sometime between 8 a.m. and 4 p.m. tomorrow.

36

Ask a friend for a lift.

37 Volunteer your time.

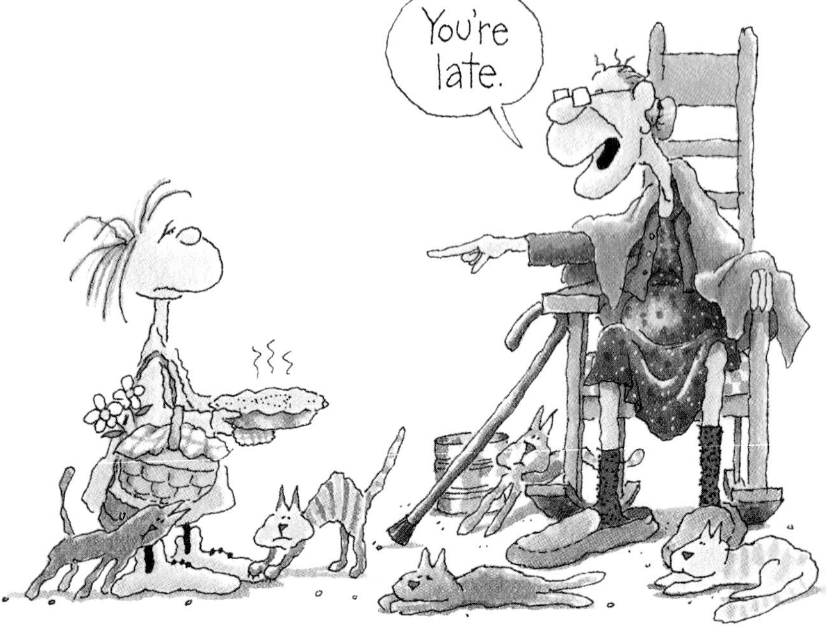
You're late.

38 Throw yourself a party!

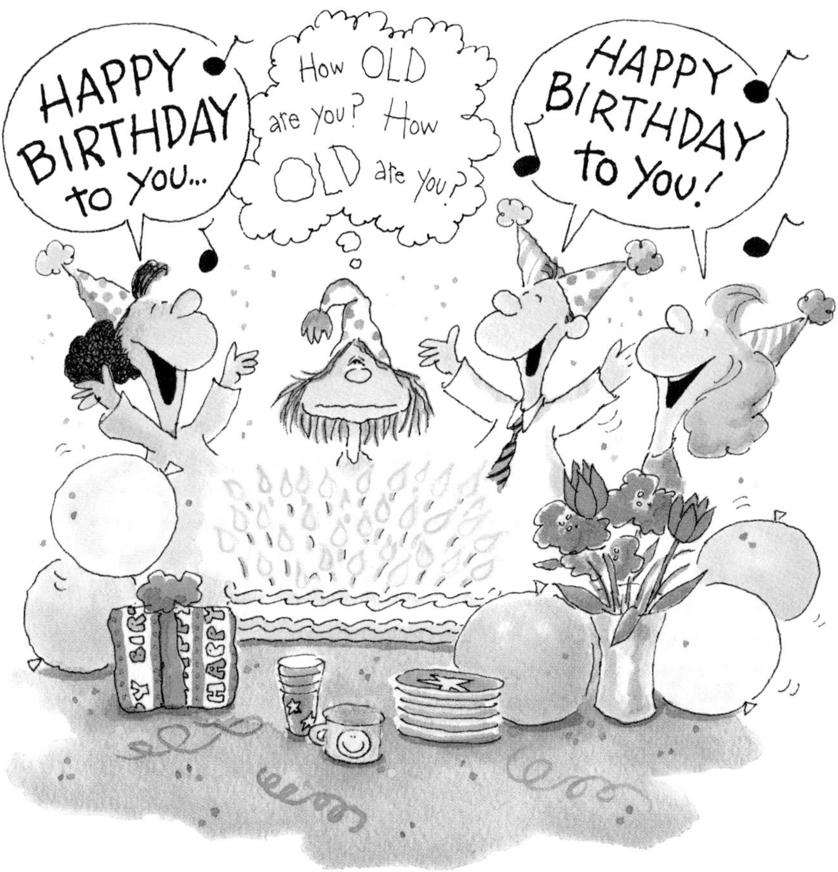
HAPPY BIRTHDAY to you...
How OLD are you? How OLD are you?
HAPPY BIRTHDAY to You!

39

Learn a new skill.

40 Buy a brand new car.

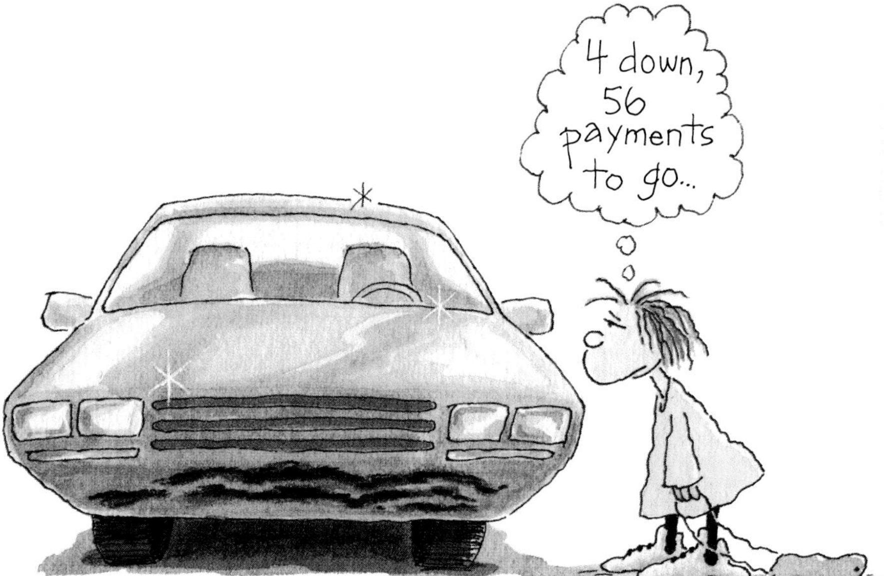
4 down, 56 payments to go...

41 Try to see the humor in things.

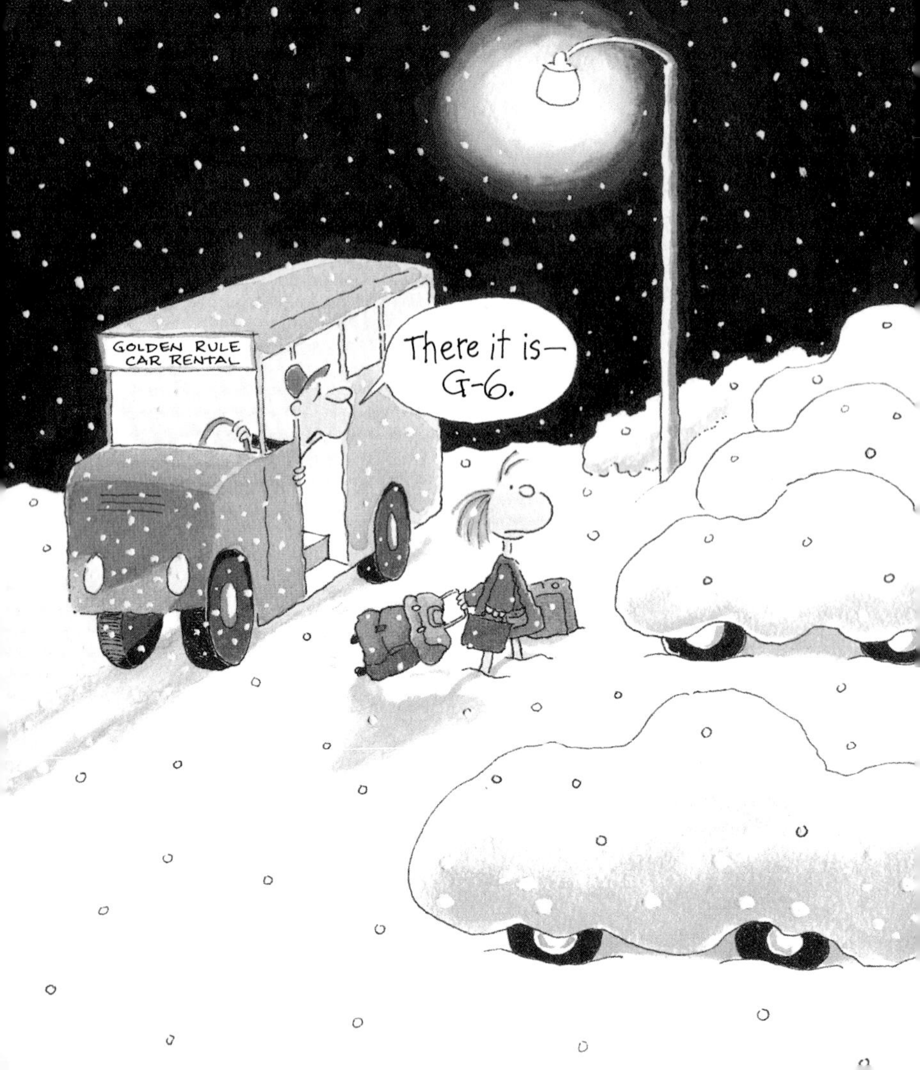
GOLDEN RULE CAR RENTAL
There it is— G-6.

42 Don't ask.

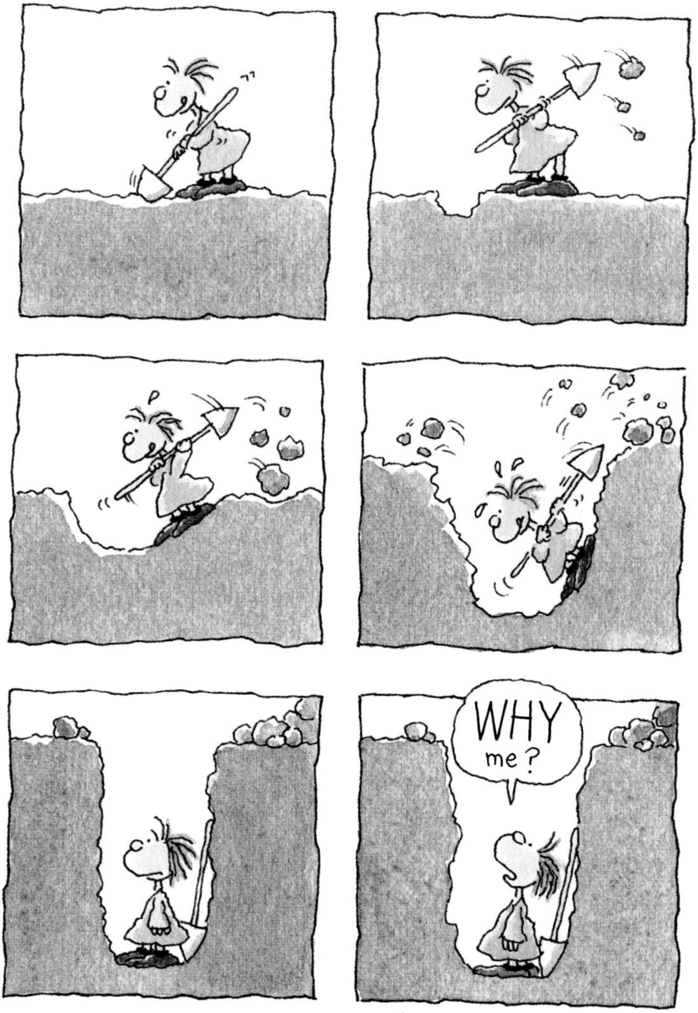
WHY
me?

43 Say "NO."

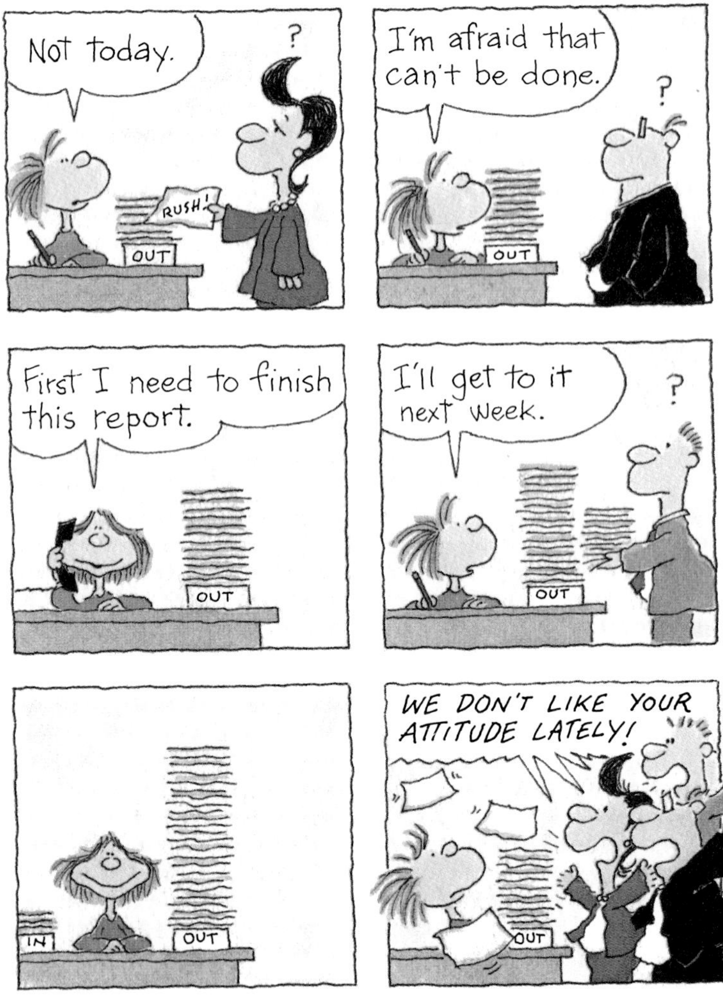
Not today.
?
RUSH!
OUT
I'm afraid that can't be done.
?
OUT
First I need to finish this report.
OUT
I'll get to it next week.
?
OUT
IN
OUT
WE DON'T LIKE YOUR ATTITUDE LATELY!
OUT

44 Extend your vacation.

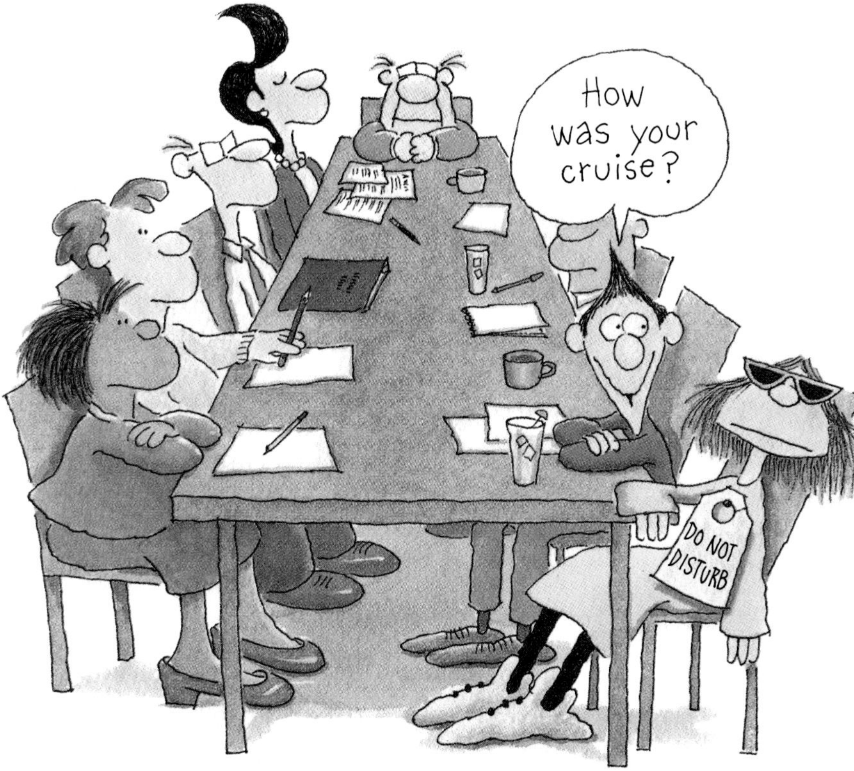
How was your cruise?
DO NOT DISTURB

45 Make a grand exit.

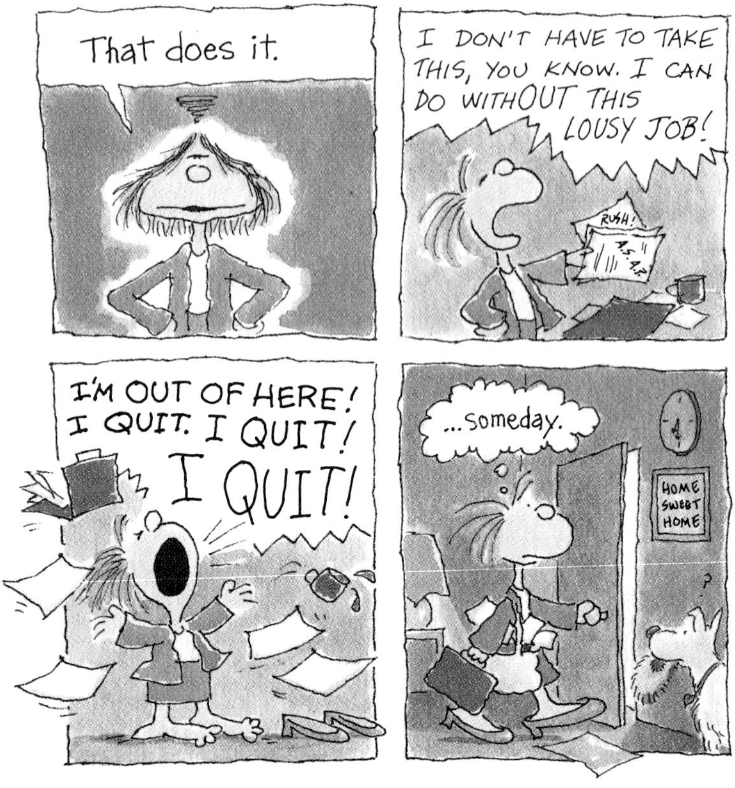
That does it.
I DON'T HAVE TO TAKE THIS, YOU KNOW. I CAN DO WITHOUT THIS LOUSY JOB!
RUSH!
A.S.A.P.
I'M OUT OF HERE! I QUIT. I QUIT! I QUIT!
...someday.
HOME SWEET HOME

46

Don't look back.

47

Accept the things you cannot change...

and change the things you cannot accept!

48 Be hopeful.

We'll
make it.

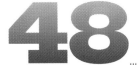

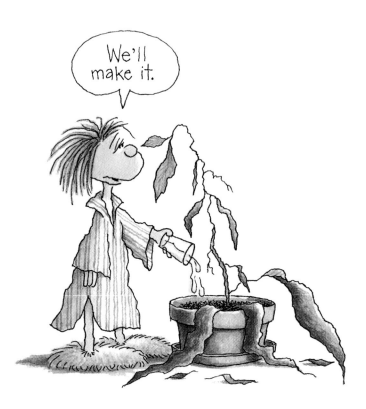

49

Do whatever gives you peace.

50 Commiserate.

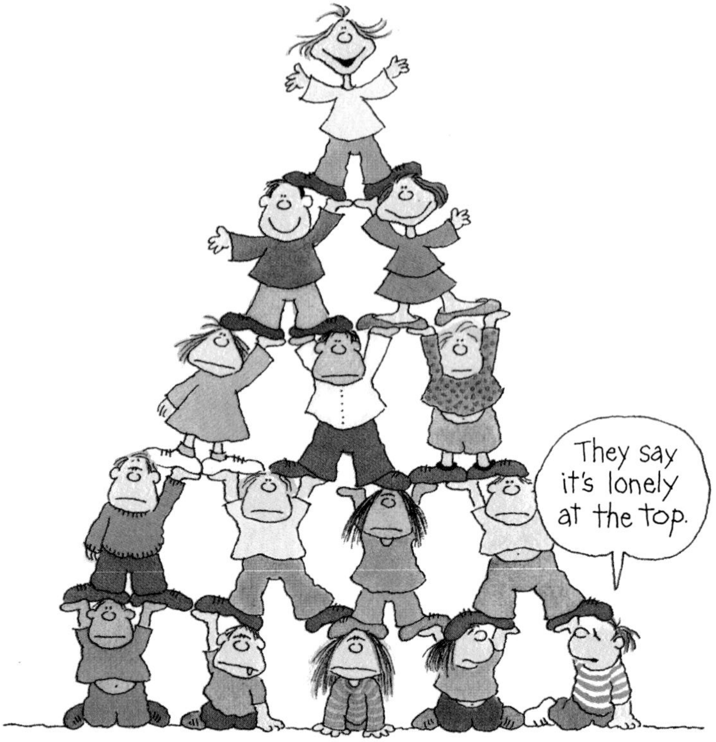
They say it's lonely at the top.

51 Make a change.

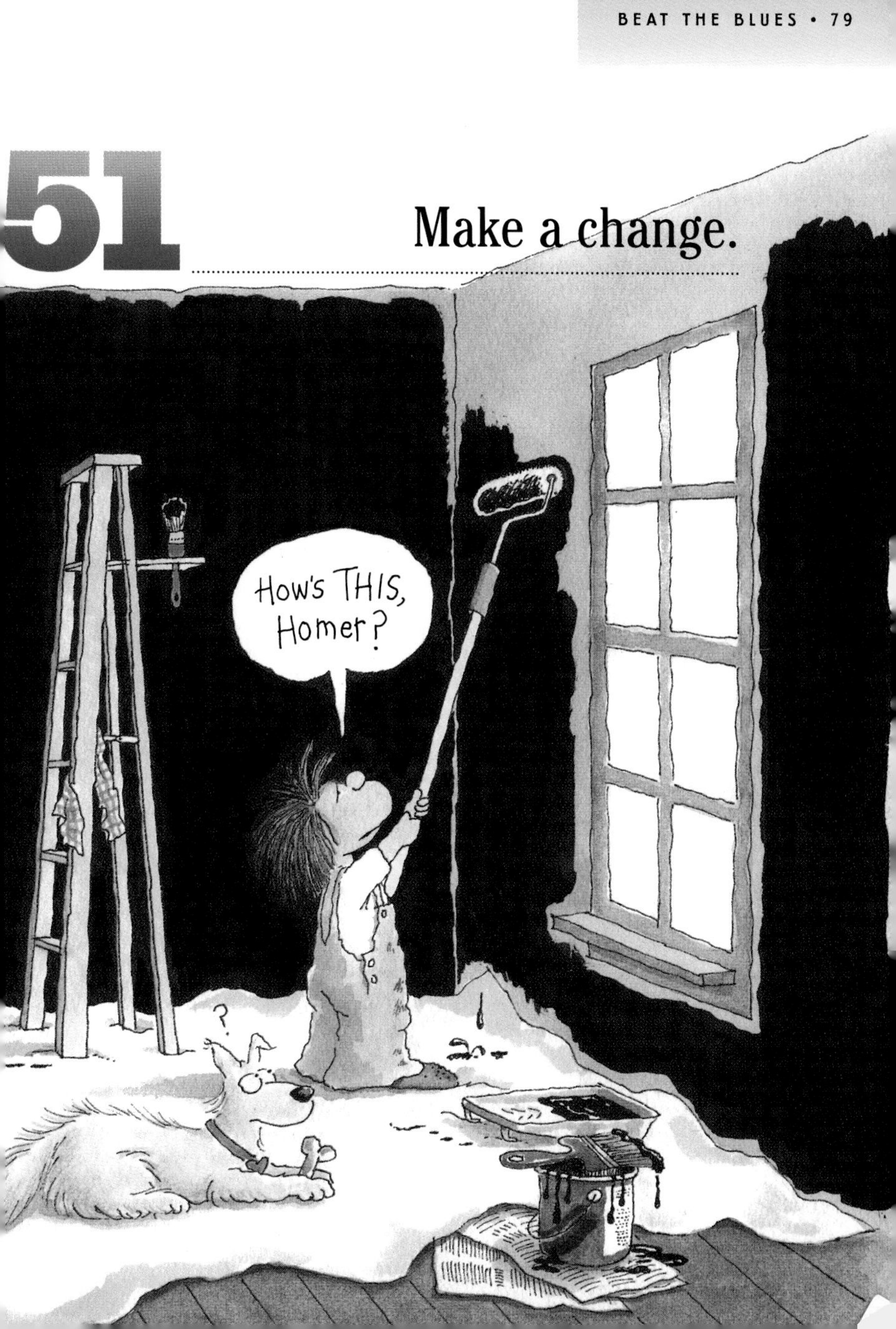
How's THIS, Homer?

52 Make rainbows.

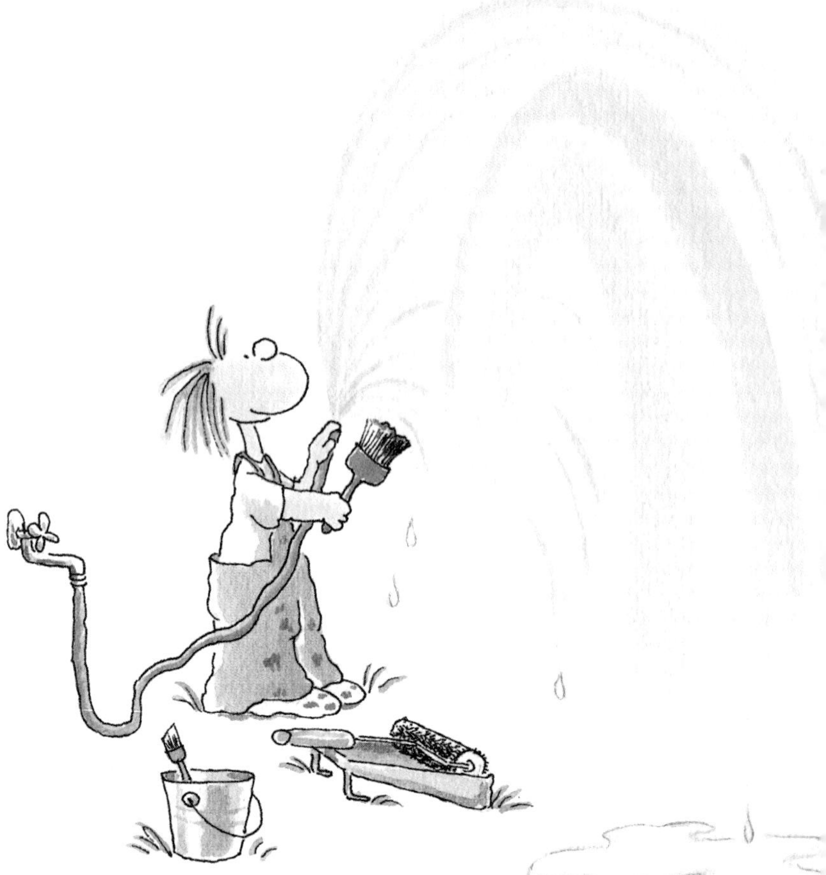

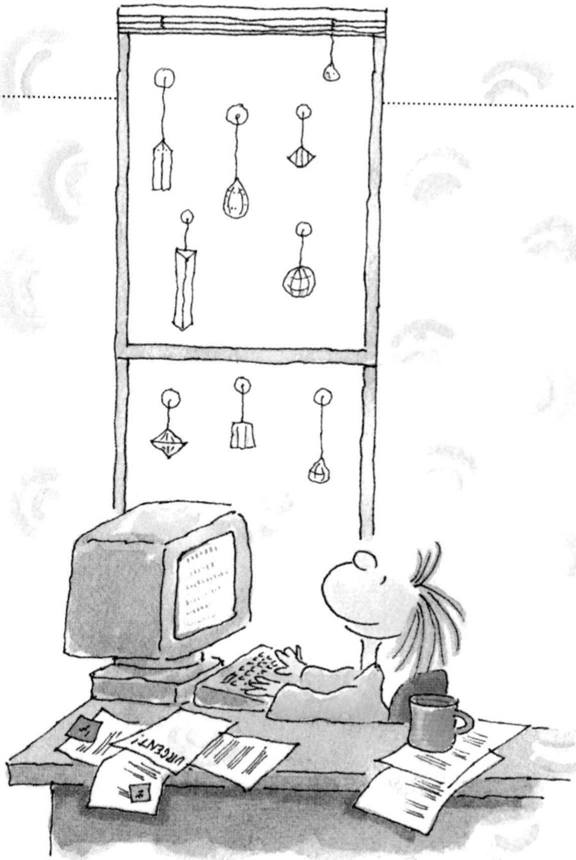
URGENT!

53 Trust your instincts.

Mind if
I join you?

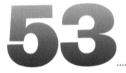

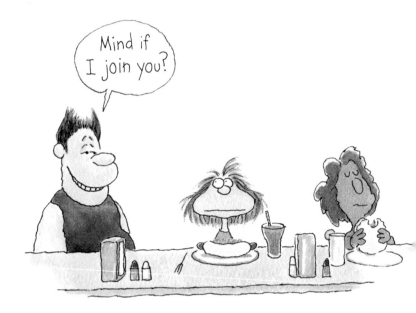

Play.

55

Find a support system.

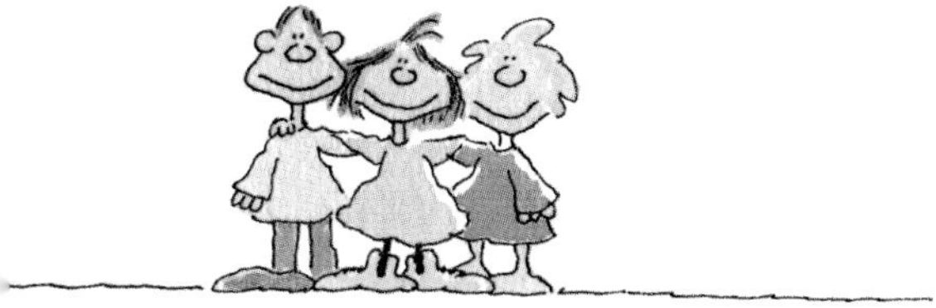

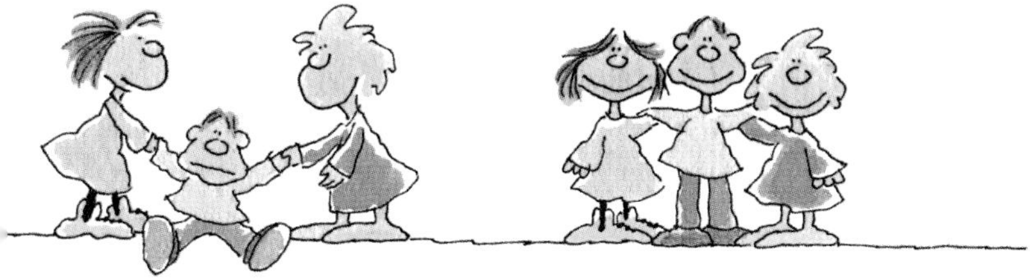

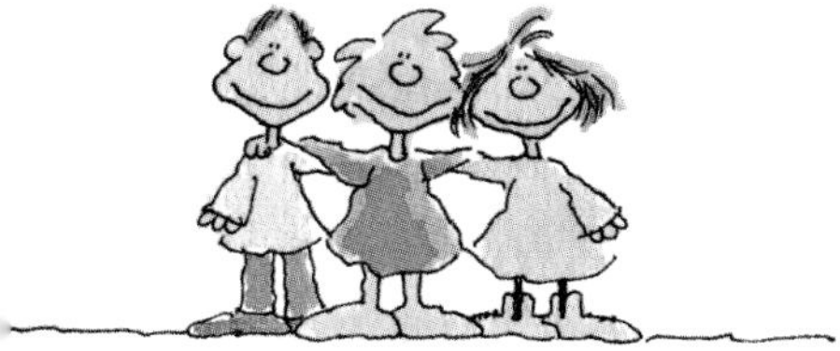

56 Get a makeover.

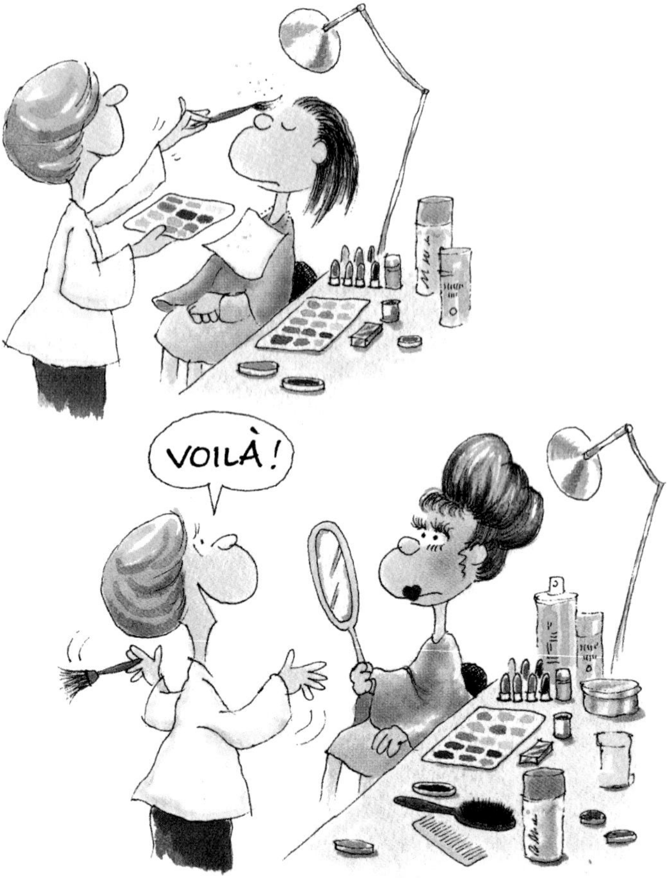
VOILÀ!

57 Change your attitude.

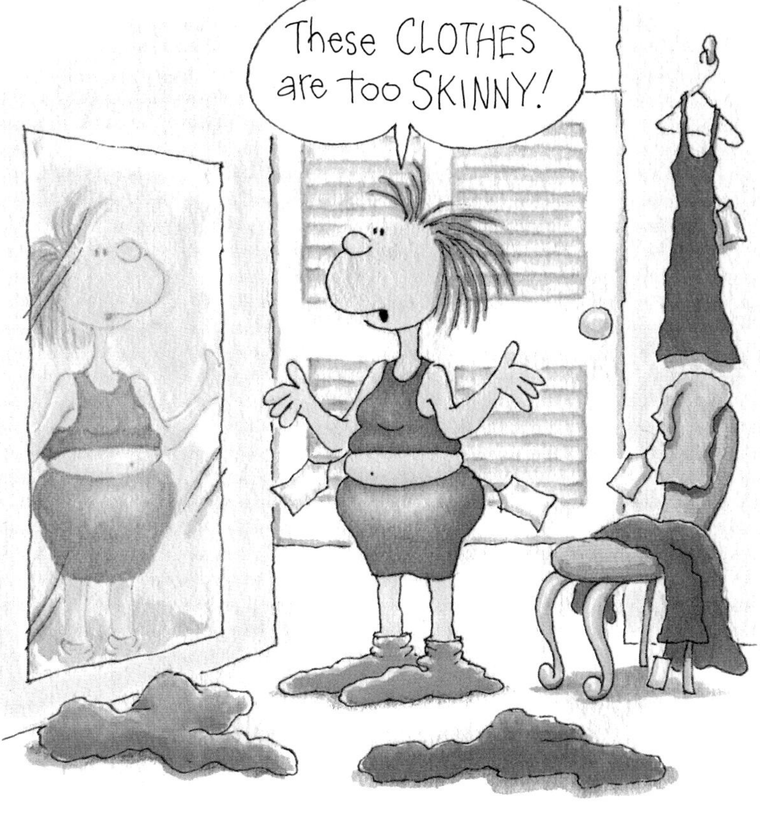
These CLOTHES
are too SKINNY!

58 Indulge yourself.

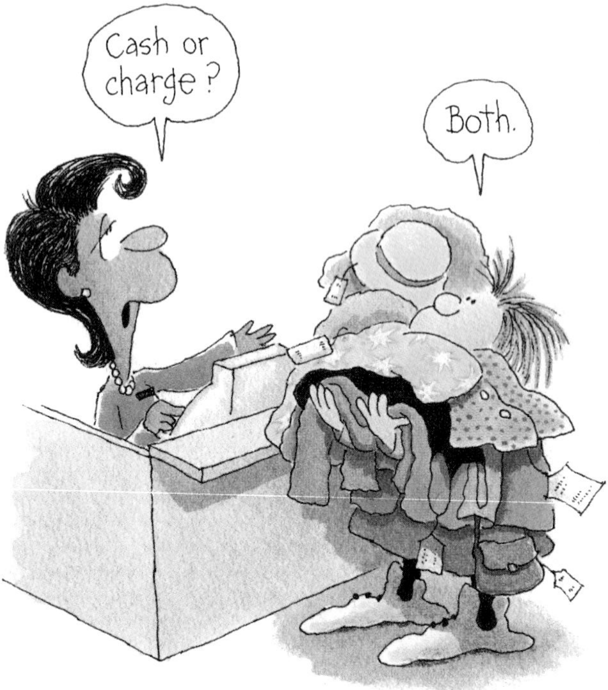
Cash or charge?
Both.

59

Drop that
fair-weather friend!

60 Take a chance.

Here. It's free.
Thank you.
It's honest. It's loyal.
Really?
It's safe. It's unselfish. It's dependable.
It is?
It's new.
Are you sure? —Wait a minute! I see a flaw.

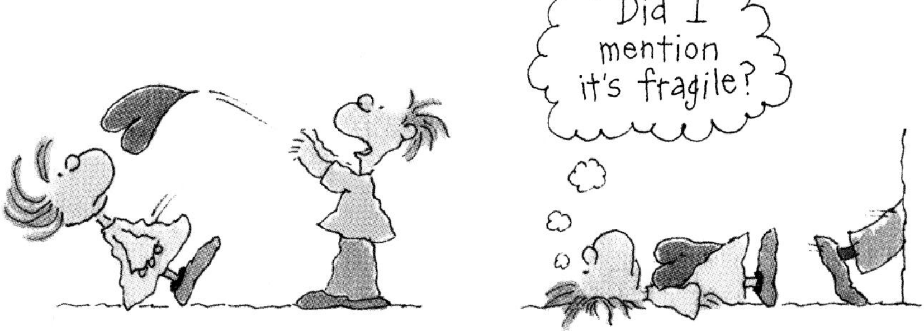
Did I
mention
it's fragile?

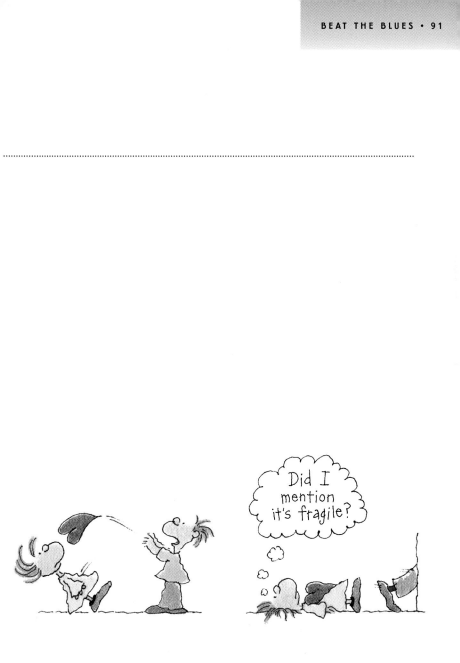

61 Make a commitment.

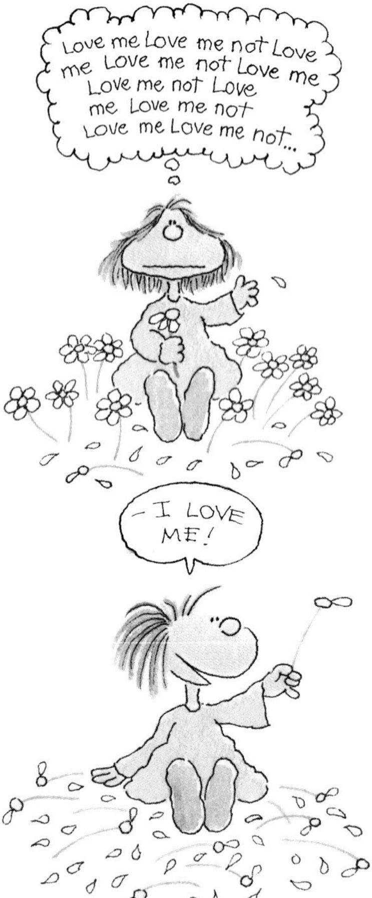
Love me Love me not Love me Love me not Love me Love me not Love me Love me not Love me Love me not...
- I LOVE ME!

62 Things aren't always as bad as they seem.

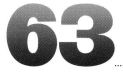

63 Don't give up!

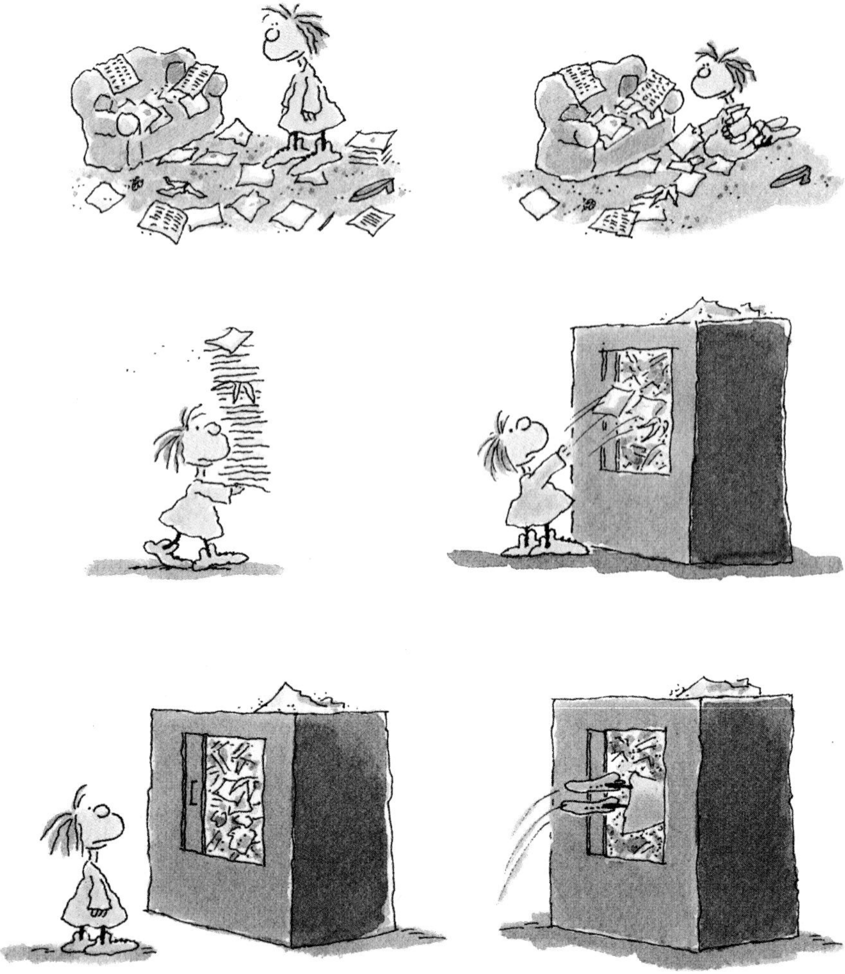

64 Think about tomorrow.

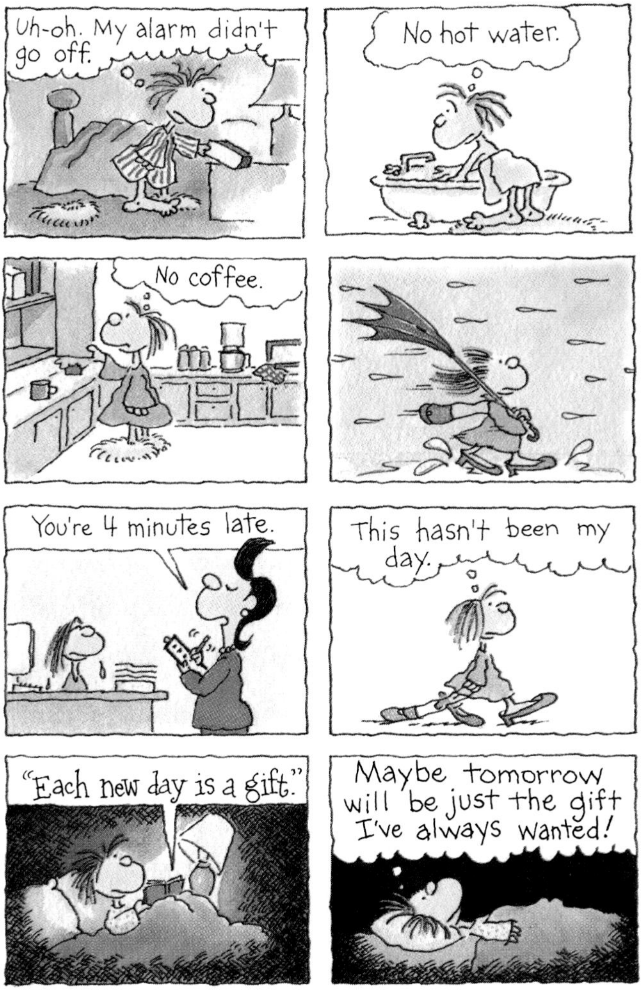
Uh-oh. My alarm didn't go off.
No hot water.
No coffee.
You're 4 minutes late.
This hasn't been my day.
"Each new day is a gift."
Maybe tomorrow will be just the gift I've always wanted!

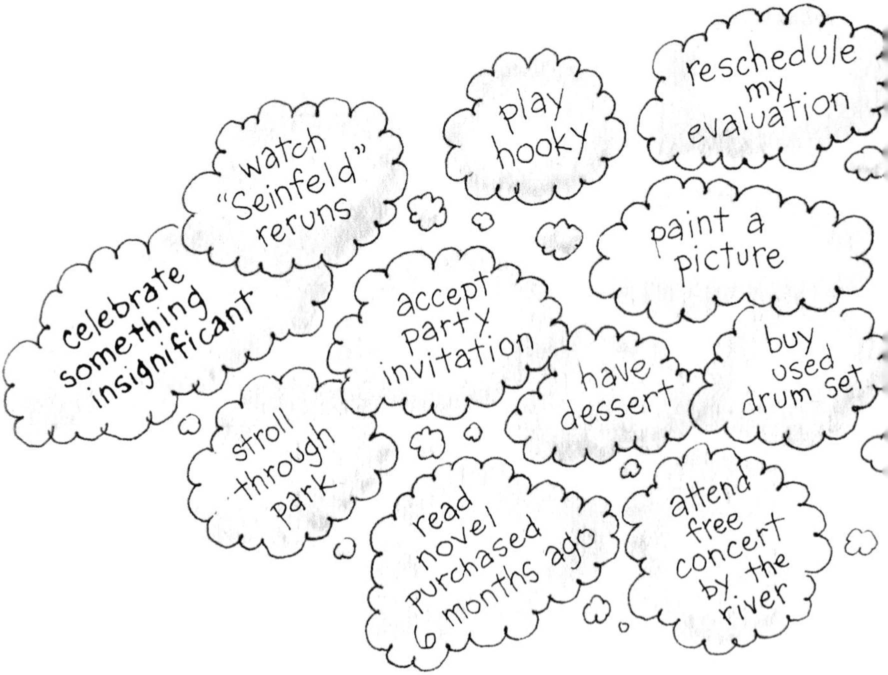
watch "Seinfeld" reruns
play hooky
reschedule my evaluation
celebrate something insignificant
accept party invitation
paint a picture
have dessert
buy used drum set
stroll through park
read novel purchased 6 months ago
attend free concert by the river